LONDON & SOUTH WESTERN LOCOMOTIVES

LONDON & SOUTH WESTERN RAILWAY COMPANY.

H. C. CASSERLEY

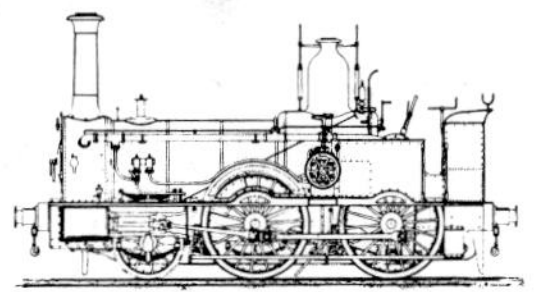

LONDON & SOUTH WESTERN LOCOMOTIVES

LONDON

IAN ALLAN

This book incorporates
LSWR LOCOMOTIVES · A SURVEY 1873-1922
by F. Burtt
published in 1949

Enlarged edition 1971

SBN 7110 0151 0

Published by Ian Allan Ltd., Shepperton, Surrey, and printed and bound in the United Kingdom by R. J. Acford Ltd., Terminus Road, Industrial Estate, Chichester, Sussex.

CONTENTS

FOREWORD

Between 1946 and 1949, the late F. Burtt, a well known expert on locomotive history of the constituent lines of the Southern Railway, produced three books dealing respectively with the engines of the London & South Western, South Eastern & Chatham, and London, Brighton & South Coast.

All of these books have long since been unobtainable, and in any case are completely out of date by now as regards the final history of their respective locomotives subsequent to publication.

The present volume, dealing with LSWR locomotives, whilst planned basically on the same pattern as Mr. Burtt's book, and incorporating much of his text, is not only considerably enlarged and brought completely up to date to the end of steam, but has in addition entirely new illustrations. Photographs are now included showing many of the variants of each engine class.

The same as its predecessor, this work finishes with locomotives built or on order up to the end of 1922, and makes no attempt to deal with new designs brought into use subsequent to the Grouping of 1923.

"Upstairs to the London & South Western's engines. . . ." The World War I memorial arch at Waterloo

INTRODUCTION

THE LONDON & SOUTH WESTERN RAILWAY

THE TWENTY or more major Railway Companies which maintained their independent existences up to the great 1923 amalgamation into four large groups were each and all utterly different from one another from any viewpoint; every one of them had its individual characteristic.

Fascinating days to those of us fortunate enough to remember them, and almost incredible to the present day generation whose shorter memory span embraces principally the last twenty years since Nationalisation, or at most some recollections of the Grouping period between the wars.

In that earlier wonderful era, now nearly half a century gone by, we railway enthusiasts of those days naturally had our own favourite amongst the larger of the railway systems. In my own case, although not at the top of the list, yet not so far down, came the London & South Western. This may have been partly due to the fact that at this time the LSWR had a very generous proportion of old engines still at work; one could not, for instance, at that time still find examples of the 1870s' vintage on many other railways. The main reason, however, was undoubtedly because at that period I lived very close to the LSWR in the London area, and was consequently able to see a good deal more of it than many other lines, particularly those in the north of England and in Scotland. In my earlier years these were a closed book so far as personal acquaintance was concerned, although I very soon learned as much about them as I could from the few railway periodicals of the time, and as regards their looks and appearance from the very lovely coloured post cards issued by the Locomotive Publishing Company, many of which are still obtainable from the present publisher.

The London & South Western was indeed a fascinating railway. At the time of the Grouping its locomotives ranged from the ancient Beatties to the very modern and up-to-date 4–6–0s of Robert Urie and its coaches were in their unusual and distinctive double livery usually described as brown and salmon. The electric coaching vehicles were dark green from the start, and the steam stock gradually followed suit. The colour of the engines at this time was bright green for the passenger and mixed traffic classes, and a dark olive green for the goods and shunting engines, of which the LSWR had a considerably smaller proportion than most other railways.

Notwithstanding the incidence of the war in 1915, the electrification of the busy London suburban routes was first embarked upon, gradually to spread further into the countryside, outwards towards Guildford and Reading, eventually in Southern Railway days to become by far the largest network of electrified lines in the country at this period. Later it was extended to the main line, Portsmouth, and quite recently to Southampton and Bournemouth also.

From a scenic point of view the LSWR could claim a not inconsiderable number of picturesque routes, the most outstanding being that charming stretch of line through the New Forest, or the lush and rolling countryside of Dorset, over which once ran the Southern Railway's 'Atlantic Coast Express', now but a memory, and the lovely journey between Exeter and Plymouth along the edge of Dartmoor, always a fascinating route. First, the continuous rise with severe gradient of 1 in 77 up to the summit of 950ft near Bridestowe, shortly after crossing the tall Meldon Viaduct over the valley of the Okement, then, once over the top, the corresponding descent the other side down into Plymouth (the approach to which was heralded by a fine view of Brunel's famous viaduct at Saltash carrying the rival GWR route over into Cornwall). Owing to weight restrictions the largest engines of the LSWR were not allowed over this route, the burden of which inevitably fell on the doughty T9 4–4–0s until after the Grouping, when they were helped out to some extent by SR N Class 2–6–0s, which were drafted to the West Country in considerable numbers.

There is much more one could say about the old London & South Western, this at best can only be the very briefest of surveys, but it is hoped that the comprehensive selection of pictures which follow will help to perpetuate the memory of what was one of the oldest established railways in the country.

In 1923 the LSWR became the largest constituent of the newly formed Southern Railway, the two other principal partners being the South Eastern & Chatham and the London, Brighton & South Coast, and the newly formed railway embraced all the counties in southern England from Kent to Devon and Cornwall with an almost complete monopoly of the area as far as Exeter. There were indeed one to two penetrations by the Great Western, such as the Didcot, Newbury & Southampton and the Weymouth lines, also the jointly owned Somerset & Dorset. Beyond Exeter, however, the LSWR was always in competition with the GWR, principally to Plymouth and Barnstaple, quite apart from the through traffic to the West of England which was for ever a thorn in the side of the Great Western. The final chapter to this lifelong rivalry has only very recently been written, when the old GWR, as the Western Region of British Railways, at last succeeded, under Beeching 'rationalisation', in getting its hooks on to its old competitor by absorbing all lines west of Salisbury, and has since proceeded systematically to close most of them. The fine main line between Salisbury and Exeter, over which once ran the 'Atlantic Coast Express', a ubiquitous train serving many destinations with individual through coaches to holiday resorts from London, has in many sections been reduced to a single track.

The LSWR originated as the London & Southampton Railway by an Act passed in 1834, authorising the construction of a line of railway from London to Southampton via Basingstoke. The first section of the line between London and Woking was opened for public traffic on the 23rd May, 1838, and on the following 24th September, to Shapley Heath: a total distance from London of 38 miles. The London terminus was situated at Nine Elms, close to Vauxhall Bridge. The original terminus with its pillared portico fronting Nine Elms Lane was in existence as a goods depot until quite recently.

Two further extensions of the railway were opened on the 10th June, 1839, from Shapley Heath (now named Winchfield) to Basingstoke—a length of eight miles, and a section of twelve miles from Southampton to Winchester. On

An old woodcut showing a very early scene on the London & Southampton Railway. The engine is a Sharp 2–2–2 of a general type which was supplied by the maker to a number of railways during this period. The LSWR ones were built in 1838, a year before the London & Southampton became the LSWR, and this view may be presumed to have depicted a scene about that time

11th May, 1840, the intermediate portion was completed and opened for public traffic, the best trains doing the journey of 79 miles between London and Southampton in three hours.

In 1839 an Act was passed, authorising a branch line to Gosport with the intention of serving Portsmouth, and the title of the company was changed to that of London & South Western Railway. The Gosport Branch was opened for traffic from Bishopstoke (now Eastleigh) on the 7th February, 1842, though some trials were made for a few days late in 1841.

The Guildford Junction Railway was acquired in 1845, forming a branch from Woking, opened 5th May, 1845.

The line from Bishopstoke to Salisbury, actually to Milford, now the Goods branch (a distance of some 22 miles) was opened for traffic on the 1st March, 1847. On the 1st June, 1847, the line from Southampton to Dorchester (a distance of 60½ miles) was opened by independent enterprise. The LSWR took it over in 1848. On 14th February, 1848, a branch from Weybridge to Chertsey was opened and on the 13th July the line was extended from Nine Elms to Waterloo.

The following are the opening dates, etc., of the more important sections:

1848	...	Fareham to Portsmouth
1848	...	Richmond to Windsor
1849	...	Guildford to Farnham
1850	...	Hounslow loop
1852	...	Farnham to Alton

1856*	...	Reading reached
1857**	...	Weymouth reached
1857	...	Salisbury reached via main line
1858	...	Brockenhurst to Lymington
1859	...	Godalming to Havant
1859†	...	Portsmouth reached via Guildford and Havant
1860	...	Exeter reached from Salisbury
1862	...	North Devon Railway (broad gauge) Crediton to Barnstaple, leased
1862	...	Ringwood to Christchurch
1865	...	Weymouth-Portland
1870	...	Ringwood to Bournemouth
1874	...	Wimbourne to Bournemouth
1874	...	Ilfracombe reached
1867–1876	...	Coleford Junction to Plymouth
1886	...	Launceston reached
1888	...	Brockenhurst-Christchurch, giving direct access to Bournemouth
1892	...	Southampton Dock Co. absorbed
1898	...	Waterloo & City 'tube' railway opened, afterwards taken over by LSWR
1895	...	Wadebridge reached, linking up with Bodmin and Wadebridge Railway (1834)
1899	...	Wadebridge to Padstow
1884–1908	...	Remaining branches
1925‡	...	North Devon and Cornwall Light Railway

* Running powers over SER

** Running powers over GWR

† Running powers over LBSCR west of Havant

‡ Opened after the Grouping by an independent Company, but worked from the start by the SR, and in practical effect a part of the old LSWR System. It was the last standard gauge passenger line of any considerable length other than certain extensions in the outer London area to be built in this country.

CHAPTER ONE

LOCOMOTIVE SUPERINTENDENTS

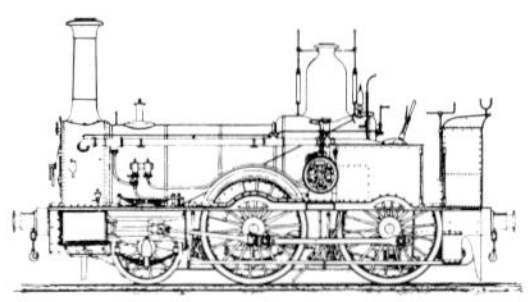

FROM A LOCOMOTIVE aspect, the history of the LSWR falls easily into five periods under the following locomotive superintendencies:

1835–1850 J. Woods and J. V. Gooch
1850–1878 Joseph Beattie and his son W. G. Beattie
1878–1895 William Adams
1895–1912 Dugald Drummond
1912–1922 Robert W. Urie

Of the earliest engines, mostly 2–2–0s, 2–2–2s and 2–4–0s built under the Woods régime, very few pictures of them have survived, but there are rather more of the Gooch engines, mostly as later rebuilt by Joseph Beattie.

During the following decade many engines were turned out by the two Beatties, father and son. Joseph Beattie, the elder, went in for numerous experiments to improve the boilers and steaming capacities of his engines, some of them producing most extraordinary appearances in the form of two separate chimneys, feed water heaters and other apparatus. Most of his express engines were of the 2–4–0 type, of considerable and fascinating variety, and it is interesting to observe that he abandoned the use of the single wheeler as early as 1859, many years before any other railway did so, (4–2–2s were even constructed as late as 1900 and 1901 by the Midland and Great Northern railways). No more express singles appeared thereafter on the LSWR, unless one accepts the non-coupled 4–2–2–0 engine built by Drummond in 1897 and 1901.

J. Beattie is probably best remembered by his 2–4–0WTs, which he introduced in 1863 for the London suburban services, and of which 85 were built between that year and 1875, the last ones coming out after his death and during the early years of his son's superintendency. They are of course well known even in recent times by virtue of the fact that although all but three of them were taken out of service as long ago as by 1898, these three were destined to survive, many times rebuilt, for more than twice as long as any of their sisters, until as recently as 1962. They were retained for this long period as being the only suitable engines for working over the Wenford Bridge mineral line in Cornwall. After 1962 it was found possible to use some small GWR 0–6–0PTs, but their reign was short lived, and they have in turn been replaced by diesels.

Two of these three interesting survivals of the past have fortunately been preserved, one by the BTC and one by the Quainton Railway Society Ltd.

Joseph Beattie also put into traffic another class, of which many were destined to enjoy long lives, although again the later survivors were of a batch which did not appear until after his death. They were double-framed 0–6–0s of a standard type of the period, built by Beyer, Peacock and were very similar to Kirtley's current design on the Midland Railway. Although withdrawn in 1913, they were laid aside but not broken up, and at the height of World War I, were reinstated to traffic in 1917 to perform several more useful years of work, not finally disappearing until 1924.

W. G. Beattie, shortly after taking over in 1871, obtained more 0–6–0s from Beyer, Peacock but this time with single frames. The later history of some of these was similar to the double framers, in that several of them which had been laid aside were given a new lease of life in 1915, and one or two lasted until 1925.

There was also a class of smaller single framed 0–6–0s, again from Beyer, Peacock known as 'Ilfracombe goods'. Two of them were broken up in 1905, but the other six had an interesting subsequent history, being sold to the renowned Colonel Stephens for use on his famous light railways, two going to the Kent & East Sussex, one to the East Kent, and three to the Shropshire & Montgomery, on which lines they survived until between 1932 and 1941.

William Adams

William Adams, born in Limehouse on 15th October, 1823, was the son of John Samuel Adams, Resident Engineer of the East and West India Dock Company. At an early age he joined the Engineering Department of the East & West India Dock Company, under his father. After a short period with Vignoles, he was apprenticed at the age of seventeen years to Miller and Ravenhill, the wellknown marine engineers, at Blackwall, where he was engaged in the erection of marine engines. In the 1840s he took a position with P. Taylor & Company at their yard at Marseilles and subsequently at Genoa, taking charge of the erection and trial runs of new marine engines.

In 1848, he was holding an important position in the engineering section of the newly formed Sardinian navy. In 1852, he returned home to England, and during the early 'fifties was engaged on various jobs, including a survey for a railway in the Isle of Wight (which did not materialise), the superintendence of docks at Cardiff, followed by the design and layout of the North London Railway workshops at Bow. He now devoted his attention to locomotive engineering, and in 1855 became the first Locomotive Superintendent of the North London Railway, on which he introduced a type of tank engine which continued as the standard wheel arrangement for the NLR's passenger traffic.

His first design was a 4–4–0 tank engine with inside cylinders, the bogie having outside frames. This was a development of a type built in 1855 by R. Stephenson & Co. for the NLR. Adams' first new engines (the 43 Class) appeared in 1863 and were the first engines built at the Bow Works. A similar but larger class (the 51 Class) came in 1865. These classes had a bogie of Adams' own design allowing a lateral movement about the pivot, and this type became standard also for the outside cylinder tanks of No 1 Class built at Bow from 1868.

In 1873, Adams left Bow to take up a similar post on the Great Eastern Railway at Stratford. On this line, however, instead of repeating his North London type, Adams continued the 0–4–4T type already introduced to the GER by S. W. Johnson, and also designed two distinctive classes of tender engine, the 4–4–0 'Ironclads' with bogies of the designer's standard type, and the

2–6–0 Mogul goods engines, both these latter classes having outside cylinders, though the tank engines did not. The first of the 2–6–0 engines was named *Mogul*, and was the first British example of that type later to become so numerous on our home railways.

In 1878, Adams quitted Stratford for the London & South Western Railway, and commenced to reign at Nine Elms, and in so doing ranked among the very few locomotive superintendents to fill the office on three English railways.

When William Adams took over he found a very miscellaneous collection of locomotives left by his predecessors, of many varying classes, and a large number of them becoming elderly and worn out. His first duty was to provide the London suburban services with some larger engines than the little 2–4–0WTs; first 12 4–4–0Ts, and later a series of 71 4–4–2T engines but with well tanks. Three of these survived the others for a long time to work the Lyme Regis branch, and one is fortunately still to be found on the Bluebell Railway.

Adams also designed several series of very fine express 4–4–0s with outside cylinders (one of which is to be seen in Clapham Museum) for main line work, also 90 0–4–2s for general mixed traffic use, 50 0–4–4Ts for suburban work, together with 60 similar but smaller engines for branch line and miscellaneous duties, many of which survived in the Isle of Wight until the end of steam there at the close of 1966.

Seventy 0–6–0s were obtained from Neilsen & Co., of which 50 went to the Middle East during World War I, never to return, but most of the remaining 20 lasted well into BR days. Adams also built other locomotives such as 0–4–0Ts and 0–6–0Ts for shunting purposes.

Until 1887, Adams obtained all his engines from contract firms, but in that year he began to build a good proportion of new requirements at the Nine Elms works (after a lapse of nearly 13 years since the last new engine), W. Pettigrew being Works Manager and an able assistant in design. The first class turned out created a sensation, being the celebrated 0–4–2 mixed traffic tender engines of the 527 Class, in a way reminiscent of Stroudley's Gladstone, with coupled wheels only six inches smaller in diameter. These 'Jubilees', as they were called, were turned out at intervals until 1895, and ultimately reached a total of 90.

In 1884, Adams decided to give compounding a trial, so he borrowed from the LNWR, F. W. Webb's 'Compound' No 300, and tried her against one of his own engines on the Exeter road. In Adams' opinion, the LNW engine was not superior to his own, but nevertheless he altered one of his 7ft 1in in 4–4–0s (No 446) to a two-cylinder compound on the Worsdell system: after three years' trial the engine was reconverted to a simple.

Until 1887, Adams' passenger tanks had been of the 4–4–2 type with outside cylinders, but thenceforward he adopted the 0–4–4 type for passenger work, the 5ft 7in 61 Class (T1) for the bigger jobs, and the 4ft 10in or 177 Class (O2) for the less important branches.

The reversing gear of Adams' engines (LSWR) was on the right hand side, and this therefore was the driver's position on the Adams footplates. Drummond and Urie engines were driven from the left, as was customary in this country with the notable exception of the GWR.

Adams was at the height of his career during the 1880s and early 1890s, but between 1893 and 1895 he began to decline, and left the LSWR in 1895. He was a great singer and musician, which gifts he retained to the last. He passed away at his residence at Putney in his eighty-first year, on 7th August, 1904.

Dugald Drummond

Born at Ardrossan, Ayrshire, on 1st January, 1840, he commenced his engineering training in 1856, at the age of sixteen years, as an apprentice in the works of Forrest and Barr, Mechanical Engineers, Glasgow, with whom he remained until 1864. During the period from 1864 to 1866, he held the position of foreman erector with the Highland Railway Company at Lochgorm Works, and was then promoted to the post of Manager of the Works. Here he was under William Stroudley and later he obtained the appointment of Works Manager at the LBSC Railway Company's Works at Brighton, again under William Stroudley.

Drummond remained at Brighton for five years, but on 1st February, 1875, returned to his native country as Locomotive Superintendent of the North British Railway at Cowlairs, Glasgow. In 1882, he accepted a similar position with the Caledonian Railway Co. at St. Rollox. In 1890, Drummond was offered a position in Australia, and in consequence resigned his office on the Caledonian Railway. The Australian appointment fell through, but Drummond was not long out of harness as he soon founded the Glasgow Railway Engineering Company with works at Govan, immediately prior to which he had set up as a consulting engineer. Among his productions at this period was a narrow gauge 0–4–0 tank engine for the Glasgow Corporation Gas Works at Dawsholm, five of which were built by Sharp, Stewart & Co., and later examples at his own Govan Works.

In August, 1895, William Adams having retired from office with the LSW Railway Company, Drummond was offered, and did not long hesitate in accepting, the post of Locomotive Superintendent, which was elevated, as from 1st January, 1905, into that of Chief Mechanical Engineer. Drummond was thus the first holder of that title on the LSWR. The Locomotive Department at Nine Elms was not long in realising that Dugald Drummond was in its midst.

His locomotives were on the whole a varied lot, but many were successful designs.

He soon reversed the practice of his predecessor in his design for express passenger engines. It will be remembered that Adams' favourite type of express engine was the four-coupled bogie engine with outside cylinders but Drummond preferred the inside cylinder 4–4–0 type, and this practice he followed to the last, by degrees increasing the power in accordance with the needs of the times. At the same time, he latterly found it necessary to adopt the 4–6–0 type for the heaviest traffic. In goods and tank engine designs, however, he followed Adams' later practice as regards wheel arrangements. One of his most successful earlier types was the M7 0–4–4T, of which 105 were built, and many of which lasted until comparatively recently. His crowning achievement was however, undoubtedly his famous T9 4–4–0s, which were in effect developments of his previous engines which he had built both for the North British and Caledonian Railways. His first ten somewhat similar engines for the LSWR were perhaps only moderately successful, but the modified design which appeared in 1899, a year later, the principal improvement of which consisted of a longer firebox, proved to be one of the most outstanding successes of locomotive design in this country for its period. Sixty-six of them were built, and they took part in main line work almost to the end of their existence. In later years they were superheated by Urie and performed even more outstanding feats, and until the coming of the SR King Arthur class engines in 1925, were regularly to be seen on top link duties on the hilly West of England route, notwithstanding the appearance of other nominally more efficient and powerful engines to take their place. Fortunately, one of them has been preserved.

Drummond also produced a smaller 5ft 7in-wheel mixed traffic version, 80 engines in all. The LSWR, with its small amount of heavy freight traffic, always felt the need of an intermediate engine in this category.

Other later and larger designs of 4–4–0 followed, quite adequate engines, but none of them attained quite the brilliance of the T9s.

When Drummond built a larger express engine in the shape of a 4–6–0, he ran into trouble when embodying four cylinders in the designs. The first of these appeared in 1905; they were massive looking machines, but proved unsatisfactory in service. They were sluggish, fired badly, and amongst other troubles frequently suffered from cracked frames owing to the awkward situation of the cylinders which were bolted to them amidships. Ten similar engines were built between 1908 and 1911, but were subject to much the same faults, and were rarely seen on the duties for which they were intended. Drummond's last ten 4–6–0s, built in 1911–12, were at least not as unsuccessful as their predecessors. Urie rebuilt them to some effect, but they had all gone by 1951.

Drummond was one of the pioneers of the four-cylinder non-compound type of locomotive. In 1897, he introduced a four-cylinder simple engine, the famous No 720, originally painted in 'Brighton' yellow, a 4–2–2–0 which embodied various distinctive features. Two inside cylinders drove on to the leading pair of driving wheels, and two outside cylinders on to the trailing pair, in outward appearance resembling to a certain extent the early Webb compounds. It was, incidentally, one of the first of three 4-cylinder designs in the country, which appeared almost concurrently, the others being G&SWR No 11 and the LNWR compound 4–4–0s. Five similar engines still with small boilers appeared in 1901. These proved to be rather more successful than the original engine, even in its rebuilt form, but none of them was ever very popular; they were only used in time of emergency.

A Drummond characteristic, first adopted on No 720 noted above, and continued on a number of classes of tender engine, was the specially designed firebox containing across it several water-tubes. They were eventually removed by Urie. Drummond was also a believer in feed water heating, and preferred a smokebox steam drier to superheating. He also introduced tenders fitted with water pick-up gear. The water troughs, however, did not materialise and the apparatus was removed.

Of Drummond's other designs, mention might be made of his 30 0–6–0s, again developments of what he had previously used on the NBR and CR, and his rail motors for branch line work, which were much in vogue during the 1900–1910 period, first his combined engine and coach and later his separate 2–2–0T engine. Most of the latter were sold to the War Department during World War I, but the three remaining engines were rebuilt as 0–4–0Ts, and were employed on shunting work in the Southampton area. There was also his private saloon, combined with engine, a 4–2–4T built in 1899. It conveyed Drummond all over the system, but was little used after his death, except for a short period in connection with the Southampton Docks extension in the 1930s. Nevertheless, it remained in Eastleigh shed right up to World War II.

On 8th November, 1912, Dugald Drummond passed away at his home in

Surbiton. The end was sudden, and there passed a locomotive engineer of outstanding, even if variable, quality.

Robert Wallace Urie

Robert Wallace Urie was born on 22nd October, 1854, and was educated at Ardeer and Glasgow. He passed through the pattern, machine and fitting shops, and gained experience as a draughtsman in general mining, hydraulic and locomotive engineering, before joining the Caledonian Railway Company as a draughtsman. In this capacity he was engaged in designing travelling cranes, etc., and was entrusted with the investigation (instituted by his chief, Drummond) of the economic effect of higher steam pressures in locomotives, and of the influence exerted by the reciprocating parts in modifying the piston steam pressures transmitted to the crank pins. Later he became chief draughtsman and subsequently Works Manager of the Caledonian Company's Works at St. Rollox, Glasgow.

In 1897, he left Glasgow to take up a similar position at Nine Elms. In November, 1912, he was appointed Chief Mechanical Engineer on the death of Drummond, and between that time and his retirement in 1922 (on the Grouping of the railways) he was responsible for the building of five classes of locomotive embodying features new to the LSWR.

Urie had very different ideas from his predecessors. The South Western still had no large express passenger engine capable of handling the heaviest trains, particularly over the West of England line. The T9s continued to perform wonders, but their capacity was necessarily limited, and a modern efficient 4–6–0 was a clear necessity. The answer was the H15 class, ten 4–6–0s of an entirely new design which came out from Eastleigh in 1914. With two outside cylinders only (Urie was not a multi-cylinder man) and high running plate almost clear of the driving wheels, they can in many ways be regarded as the forerunners of final development of steam as practised in this country. Urie rebuilt some of Drummond's unsuccessful 4–6–0s to the same pattern, and followed them with his first 4–6–0 express design, the 736 Class, later incorporated into and perpetuated by Maunsell in the King Arthurs.

In 1920, he put into service a 4–6–0 goods engine with 21in × 28in cylinders and 5ft 7in coupled wheels. In the following year he introduced two new types to the LSWR, viz. a 4–8–0 tank having 22in × 28in cylinders and 5ft 1in coupled wheels, followed by a 4–6–2 tank with 21in × 28in cylinders and 5ft 7in coupled wheels. The 4–8–0Ts were for hump shunting in Feltham Marshalling Yard. The 4–6–2Ts were chiefly employed on local freight work.

In his H15 mixed traffic engines of 1914, he tried out various superheaters and compared their efficiency with saturated engines of the same batch and eventually designed and adopted the Eastleigh superheater as standard, which it remained till Maunsell's time.

The Urie engines ranked among the most advanced and efficient on British railways. They were distinctive in appearance and noteworthy in their capabilities. When the Grouping brought about Urie's retirement from the mechanical sphere of railway activity, there went one of the most able locomotive engineers who have occupied positions in the front rank of that branch of railway operation in England. Urie died at Largs on 6th January, 1937, in his 83rd year.

CHAPTER TWO

LOCOMOTIVE OVERTURE

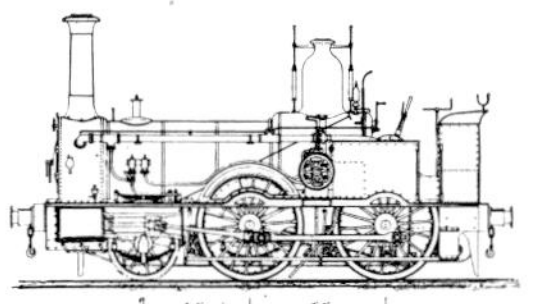

Power Classification

In 1916, Urie introduced a power classification denoted by the use of letters of the alphabet, 'A' representing the highest power down to 'K' the lowest. The letters were painted at the front end of the footplate angle iron just behind the buffer beam, or on the combined sandbox and splasher on some of the older engines.

The Duplicate List

When an engine was replaced without being scrapped a cypher was prefixed to the number and new number plates were cast as required. This practice ceased in Drummond's time, though a few engines in 1896–1901 had new plates of the Adams' pattern, notably 0282, an Ilfracombe goods and 0314, a Beattie Well Tank, to give only two examples. Drummond's policy was, at first, to remove the number plate, if any, apply transfer numerals and paint a cancelling line through these. If the engine bore the individual brass numerals, the cancelling line was painted across them but this proved troublesome and the cancellation line therefore came to be painted underneath the number, and from a line it soon degenerated into a dot that made it hardly possible to tell a duplicate list loco. at sight. In the office records, however, and generally on the actual motion parts, including coupling rods, the cypher was always used. On certain engines, such as those withdrawn but reinstated for further service during the war period 1914–18, the suffix 'A' was used, and it appeared again just after the Grouping. Then the cypher 'O' was again used until 1931, when 3000 was added to the old number as engines went through the shops.

Incidentally, the reinstatement of locomotives abovementioned gave rise to the curious position that some of their duplicate numbers had meantime been re-allotted to fresh duplicate engines, so that their restoration to service created what was virtually a 'triplicate' list. Among others, the numbers 277/88, 307/10/2/37/47/70 might each be found on no fewer than 3 engines concurrently. The engines thus reprieved were mainly, if not exclusively, old Beattie 0–6–0 goods, both single-framed and double-framed.

The practice of placing engines on the duplicate list was continued after the Grouping with engines 473–478, which became 0473–0478, 521/2/4, altered to 0521/2/4 and 449 to 0449. The last mentioned was a Drummond 4–6–0, retained for a few years for experimental purposes, as described later, and it was altered to 0449 to avoid confusion with the new SR King Arthurs. After this the practice virtually ceased, except that as late as 1942, Adams 0–4–2 No 555 was altered to 3555 for a few days only (duplicate engines by this time having a '3' prefix instead of the former 'O'). This was in anticipation of the construction of new Bulleid 0-6-0s for the SR, intended to be 550–589, but which in fact came out as C1–C40, so that 3555 reverted to 555.

Locomotives Built at Nine Elms Works

While Gooch was Locomotive Superintendent, thirty-four engines were built in the Company's Works between 1843 and 1850.

The next 126 engines built as Nine Elms had works numbers allotted starting at 1, so that engine with works number 126 was the 243rd built there. In the following list, the works numbers are bracketed:

1862	Nos. 27, 28, 50, 107 (1 to 4)	4	121
1863	Nos. 67, 78, 55, 56, 57, 29, 69, 71 (5 to 12), 68 (19), 72 (21) ...	10	131
1864	Nos. 101, 102, 103, 73, 74, 75 (13 to 18), 70 (20)	7	138
1865	Nos. 52, 53, 54, 77 (22 to 25), 79, 80, 81 (27 to 29)	7	145
1866/7	Nos. 82 (26), 58, 59, 60, 63, 64, 66, 83, 84, 85, 92, 93, 94, 86, 87, 88 (30 to 44)	16	161
1868	Nos. 89, 90, 91, 95, 96, 97, 98, 99, 100 (45 to 53)	9	170
1869	Nos. 108 to 113, 61, 62, 114, to 117, 119, 121, 122 (54 to 68) ...	15	185
1870	Nos. 65, 120, 176, 1, 14, 15, 3, 7, 8, 2, 4, 6, 9, 10 (69 to 82) ...	14	199
1871	Nos. 12, 13, 22, 38, 18, 19, 20, 17, 21, 23, 24, 33, 36, 76 (83 to 96)	14	213
	Completion of J. Beattie's orders by W. G. Beattie:		
1872	25, 26, 118, 16, 271, 272 (97 to 102)	6	219
1873	5, 11, 31, 279, 280, 281, 32, 35, 294, 291, 292, 293 (103 to 114) ...	12	231
1874	37, 39, 40, 295, 296, 297, 315, 316, 317, 41, 42 (115 to 125) ...	11	242
1875	43 (126)	1	243

No more engines were built at Nine Elms Works until 1887, after which production continued steadily until 1908 when the works were transferred to Eastleigh. The following table lists all engines built at Nine Elms during this period.

Works No	*Loco No*	*Works No*	*Loco No*	*Works No*	*Loco No*	*Works No*	*Loco No*
244	527	**265**	62	**286**	554	**307**	189
245	528	**266**	63	**287**	555	**308**	190
246	529	**267**	64	**288**	556	**309**	191
247	530	**268**	65	**289**	75	**310**	192
248	531	**269**	66	**290**	178	**311**	193
249	532	**270**	67	**291**	179	**312**	578
250	533	**271**	68	**292**	180	**313**	194
251	534	**272**	68	**293**	76	**314**	579
252	535	**273**	70	**294**	181	**315**	580
253	536	**274**	71	**295**	182	**316**	195
254	537	**275**	72	**296**	183	**317**	581
255	538	**276**	547	**297**	77	**318**	196
256	539	**277**	548	**298**	184	**319**	582
257	540	**278**	549	**299**	185	**320**	583
258	541	**279**	73	**300**	577	**321**	584
259	61	**280**	74	**301**	186	**322**	585
260	542	**281**	550	**302**	78	**323**	586
261	543	**282**	551	**303**	79	**324**	197
262	544	**283**	552	**304**	80	**325**	198
263	545	**284**	177	**305**	187	**326**	199
264	546	**285**	553	**306**	188	**327**	200

Works No	*Loco No*	*Works No*	*Loco No*	*Works No*	*Loco No*	*Works No*	*Loco No*
328	201	**388**	571	**448**	236	**507**	251
329	202	**389**	572	**449**	652	**508**	252
330	203	**390**	573	**450**	653	**509**	253
331	204	**391**	176	**451**	654	**510**	720
332	205	**392**	574	**452**	655	**511**	254
333	206	**393**	575	**453**	656	**512**	255
334	85	**394**	81	**454**	11	**513**	256
335	587	**395**	95	**455**	12	**514**	667
336	588	**396**	96	**456**	12	**515**	668
337	589	**397**	576	**456**	13	**516**	669
338	207	**398**	97	**457**	14	**517**	670
339	208	**399**	98	**458**	15	**518**	671
340	590	**400**	597	**459**	16	**519**	672
341	209	**401**	598	**460**	677	**520**	673
342	210	**402**	99	**461**	17	**521**	674
343	591	**403**	100	**462**	18	**522**	675
344	86	**404**	599	**463**	678	**523**	676
345	87	**405**	600	**464**	19	**524**	271
346	592	**406**	102	**465**	20	**525**	272
347	211	**407**	103	**466**	679	**526**	273
348	593	**408**	601	**467**	657	**527**	274
349	594	**409**	602	**468**	680	**528**	275
350	595	**410**	603	**469**	658	**529**	31
351	212	**411**	604	**470**	681	**530**	32
352	596	**412**	605	**471**	659	**531**	33
353	213	**413**	1	**472**	682	**532**	34
354	214	**414**	606	**473**	660	**533**	35
355	215	**415**	2	**474**	661	**534**	36
356	215	**416**	3	**475**	662	**535**	37
357	217	**417**	4	**476**	683	**536**	38
358	218	**418**	5	**477**	684	**537**	39
359	219	**419**	257	**478**	663	**538**	40
360	220	**420**	6	**479**	685	**539**	290
361	221	**421**	7	**480**	664	**540**	291
362	222	**422**	8	**481**	686	**541**	292
363	88	**423**	258	**482**	665	**542**	293
364	223	**424**	9	**483**	666	**543**	294
365	224	**425**	10	**484**	358	**544**	237
366	89	**426**	259	**485**	359	**545**	238
367	225	**427**	260	**486**	360	**546**	239
368	90	**428**	261	**487**	361	**547**	295
369	226	**429**	262	**488**	362	**548**	240
370	91	**430**	263	**489**	363	**549**	279
371	557	**431**	264	**490**	364	**550**	296
372	92	**432**	265	**491**	365	**551**	297
373	558	**433**	266	**492**	366	**552**	298
374	93	**434**	647	**493**	367	**553**	299
375	559	**435**	648	**494**	267	**554**	22
376	94	**436**	649	**495**	268	**555**	23
377	560	**437**	227	**496**	269	**556**	24
378	561	**438**	228	**497**	270	**557**	25
379	562	**439**	229	**498**	242	**558**	26
380	563	**440**	230	**499**	243	**559**	41
381	564	**441**	231	**500**	244	**560**	42
382	565	**442**	650	**501**	245	**561**	43
383	566	**443**	232	**502**	246	**562**	44
384	567	**444**	233	**503**	247	**563**	733
385	568	**445**	234	**504**	248	**564**	241
386	569	**446**	651	**505**	249	**565**	113
387	570	**447**	235	**506**	250	**566**	114

Works No	*Loco No*	*Works No*	*Loco No*	*Works No*	*Loco No*	*Works No*	*Loco No*
567	115	**626**	340	**685**	398	**744**	46
568	116	**627**	341	**686**	399	**745**	47
569	117	**628**	343	**687**	400	**746**	48
570	118	**629**	342	**688**	159	**747**	49
571	119	**630**	344	**689**	161	**748**	50
572	120	**631**	345	**690**	163	**749**	3*
573	121	**632**	347	**691**	164	**750**	4*
574	122	**633**	393	**692**	165	**751**	51
575	280	**634**	394	**693**	401	**752**	5*
576	281	**635**	380	**694**	402	**753**	6*
577	282	**636**	381	**695**	403	**754**	7*
578	283	**637**	382	**696**	404	**755**	52
579	284	**638**	383	**697**	21	**756**	8*
580	285	**639**	384	**698**	27	**757**	53
581	286	**640**	385	**699**	28	**758**	9*
582	287	**641**	386	**700**	29	**759**	54
583	288	**642**	387	**701**	30	**760**	10*
584	289	**643**	388	**702**	108	**761**	55
585	160	**644**	389	**703**	109	**762**	11*
586	162	**645**	390	**704**	110	**763**	56
587	276	**646**	391	**705**	111	**764**	57
588	277	**647**	392	**706**	134	**765**	58
589	278	**648**	135	**707**	148	**766**	59
590	348	**649**	136	**708**	166	**767**	60
591	349	**650**	137	**709**	167	**768**	330
592	351	**651**	138	**710**	168	**769**	331
593	353	**652**	139	**711**	1*	**770**	332
594	354	**653**	140	**712**	2*	**771**	333
595	112	**654**	141	**713**	379	**772**	334
596	318	**655**	142	**714**	415	**773**	12*
597	319	**656**	143	**715**	416	**774**	13*
598	320	**657**	144	**716**	417	**775**	174
599	321	**658**	145	**717**	418	**776**	175
600	322	**659**	146	**718**	419	**777**	407
601	323	**660**	149	**719**	169	**778**	408
602	324	**661**	150	**720**	170	**779**	409
603	356	**662**	151	**721**	171	**780**	14*
604	357	**663**	152	**722**	172	**781**	15*
605	300	**664**	153	**723**	173	**782**	410
606	301	**665**	123	**724**	420	**783**	411
607	302	**666**	124	**725**	421	**784**	412
608	303	**667**	130	**726**	422	**785**	413
609	304	**668**	132	**727**	423	**786**	414
610	305	**669**	133	**728**	424	**787**	736
611	307	**670**	374	**729**	425	**788**	405
612	369	**671**	375	**730**	426	**789**	406
613	310	**672**	376	**731**	427	**790**	737
614	311	**673**	377	**732**	428	**791**	435
615	312	**674**	378	**733**	429	**792**	738
616	313	**675**	Jt.1*	**734**	430	**793**	739
617	314	**676**	Jt.2*	**735**	431	**794**	436
618	370	**677**	154	**736**	432	**795**	740
619	371	**678**	155	**737**	433	**796**	741
620	372	**679**	156	**738**	434	**797**	437
621	373	**680**	157	**739**	104	**798**	742
622	336	**681**	158	**740**	105	**799**	743
623	337	**682**	395	**741**	106	**800**	744
624	338	**683**	396	**742**	107	**801**	745
625	329	**684**	397	**743**	45	**802**	438

* Rail Motor

Works No	*Loco No*	*Works No*	*Loco No*	*Works No*	*Loco No*	*Works No*	*Loco No*
803	439	**807**	335	**811**	747	**815**	82
804	440	**808**	453	**812**	455	**816**	83
805	441	**809**	746	**813**	456	**817**	84
806	442	**810**	454	**814**	457		

Eastleigh Works Numbers

The following record is no more than a carefully calculated one, as no official list has ever been issued. The first 47 numbers are easy enough to compute, but it is at that stage that one runs into difficulties, the point being whether the renewal of engines 330–335 should be regarded as rebuilds or new construction. As the engines went into the works and duly emerged in their new form incorporating parts of the old ones it is felt that on the whole they should be regarded merely as rebuilds, although some authorities prefer to classify them otherwise. The case of the 453 Class 4–6–0s is entirely different as in this instance the new locomotives were actually out and in service whilst the old ones which they replaced were still lying in Eastleigh yard, minus their tenders (which were in fact transferred to the new King Arthurs). No part of the engines themselves, however, could have been incorporated into the new locomotives, and for this reason they can hardly be counted as 'rebuilds'. Moreover one of them, duly renumbered in the duplicate list as 0449 (almost the last occasion on which this long established procedure was carried out on the LSWR), remained in service for another two years concurrently with the new 449.

The late F. Burtt was amongst those who preferred to count Nos 330–335 as new engines as they had new frames, and it will be seen that they are thus allowed for in his table of Eastleigh Works numbers, which is therefore reproduced on this basis to avoid complications, although not strictly in accordance with the present author's own ideas. It is suitably brought up to date with later additions.

Further particular of all the foregoing engines can be found by reference to the detailed lists on the following pages.

Works No	*Loco No*	*Works No*	*Loco No*
1	101	**14**	126
2	147	**15**	127
3	448	**16**	128
4	449	**17**	129
5	450	**18**	131
6	451	**19**	328
7	452	**20**	479
8	443	**21**	480
9	444	**22**	481
10	445	**23**	458
11	446	**24**	460
12	447	**25**	463
13	125	**26**	461

Works No	*Loco No*	*Works No*	*Loco No*
27	462	**70**	508
28	464	**71**	509
29	459	**72**	510
30	465	**73**	511
31	466	**74**	512
32	467	**75**	513
33	468	**76**	514
34	469	**77**	515
35	470	**78**	496
36	471	**79**	492
37	472	**80**	493
38	486	**81**	494
39	487	**82**	495
40	482	**83**	516
41	483	**84**	517
42	488	**85**	518
43	484	**86**	519
44	489	**87**	520
45	485	**88**	746
46	490	**89**	747
47	491	**90**	748
48	335†	**91**	749
49	736	**92**	750
50	737	**93**	751
51	738	**94**	752
52	739	**95**	753
53	740	**96**	754
54	741	**97**	755
55	742	**98**	473
56	743	**99**	474
57	744	**100**	475
58	745	**101**	476
59	497	**102**	477
60	498	**103**	478
61	499	**104**	521
62	500	**105**	522
63	501	**106**	523
64	502	**107**	524
65	503	**108**	330†
66	504	**109**	331†
67	505	**110**	332†
68	506	**111**	333†
69	507	**112**	334†

† These engines were actually 'rebuilds' or 'renewals', although classified as new construction for the purpose of this table.

Liveries

Beattie's livery until the 1860s was a decidedly plain crimson, which he afterwards changed to umber, with black bands and orange and bright green lining. In 1885, Adams adopted pea green with white lines and black edging for express engines, and holly green with light green lines and black edging for all other classes. In 1887 the pea green was extended to all passenger types, the darker green being retained for goods engines, and elliptical brass number plates with raised characters were adopted on all new engines and on many rebuilds showing

LSWR and *Southern styles of lettering, numerals and liveries (small panels) as displayed at Eastleigh*

build or rebuild date as well as the engine number; the background was bright red. From 1879 to 1887 individual brass numerals were used, each one pinned on in place, and the date plates were those of the contractors who built the various engines. Soon after Drummond took office he introduced the smooth elliptical brass number plates associated with his Scottish engines. He also changed the black edging to brown with black bands flanked by a white line each side, and this continued during the early Urie period, but the shade of green was considerably darkened. In 1918, black edging with a single white

Experimental style of livery in 1931, never brought into use

line was adopted. The dark green was retained for goods engines until 1923. The Drummond number plate was abolished in the summer of 1903, and thereafter he used plain transfer numerals commonly called 'painted on'.

After Grouping the new formed SR displayed the word SOUTHERN in full on the tender or tank sides. with the engine number in large figures beneath. This practice continued till 1938, when the number began to appear on the cabside instead of the tender, the LMSR and LNER having already discovered some years previously that if an engine borrowed a tender not its own for some reason confusion was likely to occur. The style of lettering was also altered considerably at the same time, as seen by the illustrative panel depicting the old and new styles. The other illustration depicts LSWR lettering style and various designs of panelling.

The shade of green was also changed again, this time to a very pleasing colour known as 'malachite', laid out in yellow and black instead of white and black, with very great improvement. Unfortunately it was destined to be very short lived, as wartime austerity soon dictated that all engines were to be painted plain black. Right to the end of its separate existence, however, SR engines continued, with a few minor exceptions, to carry the name SOUTHERN in full.

The only ones which did not conform were the B4 dock tanks which were named, and the 4–2–4T Inspection Cab which had just plain SR when repainted in 1932.

In 1931, also, the tender of 0–4–2 No 553 was experimentally painted S 553 R, as illustrated but this contemplated new style was never adopted.

CHAPTER THREE

THE BEATTIE ENGINES

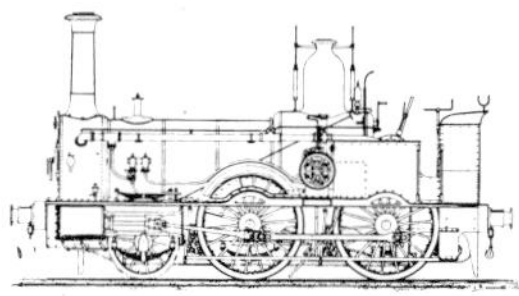

AT THE FORMATION of the Southern Railway in 1923, the LSWR contributed to the pool 912 engines of 13 wheel-types, exclusive of Drummond's 4–2–4 Inspection Cab, and amongst this stock-in-trade was a fair number of Beattie productions. One such class that still exists comprised three of the elder Beattie's 2–4–0 well-tanks, once so numerous and familiar in suburban London. There were also two 0–6–0 freight classes which are generally ascribed to Beattie the younger, though it seems certain that his father had been responsible for their design. In addition, all the well-known 0–6–0 saddle tanks supplied to W. G. Beattie's order by Beyer, Peacock were still in service and were taken into the SR stock, together with sundry odd engines of the same pre-Adams periods.

Hence, although this summarised history is aimed principally at those LSWR engines which Adams and his successors brought out until 1923, the survivors mentioned above must briefly be reviewed in order to complete the picture.

The North Devon Railway, which eventually became part of the LSWR system, was constructed to the 7ft 0in broad gauge. It was worked by very miscellaneous collection of locomotives, one of which was this Crewe type 2–4–0, Creedy. *The North Devon was purchased by the LSWR in 1865 and was converted to mixed gauge in 1870, but broad gauge working lasted until 1877, when* Creedy *was withdrawn. It is worth noting that the line between Exeter and Crediton was also mixed gauge at this period*

Tartar, *a 2–2–2WT built by Sharp Bros in 1852, one of a class of six. Withdrawn in 1873*

No 153 Victoria, *the last express single wheeler built for the LSWR, was turned out from Nine Elms in 1859. Later rebuilt as a 2–4–0, it was scrapped in 1884*

No 69 Argus, *one of Joseph Beattie's many series of 2–4–0s. One of the Falcon Class, it was turned out from Nine Elms works in 1863; withdrawn 1886. The view is believed to have been taken at Salisbury in 1864*

Beattie 2–4–0 No 75 Fireking, *one of a series of 7ft 0in 2–4–0s built at Nine Elms, this particular one in 1864 (withdrawn 1888)*

Gooch built a series of fifteen 2–4–0s mainly for goods work, of which No 41 Ajax *was turned out from Nine Elms in 1855. It was later the subject of Joseph Beattie's experimental gadgets, shown here. Withdrawn in 1883*

A rare early view of a Beattie 2–4–0 working a train. No 0236 (built by Beyer, Peacock in 1866, and withdrawn in 1899), at an unidentified location

One of Beattie's 2–4–0s as later modified by Adams in 1888, having been originally built at Nine Elms in 1870. It lasted until 1895

Vesuvius Class 2–4–0 No 294, built at Nine Elms in 1873, seen here in its later days with an Adams chimney, in the repair bay at Bournemouth shed. The engine was withdrawn in 1899

One of Joseph Beattie's 0–6–0s, Lion Class, No 3 Transit, *built at Nine Elms in 1870. It lasted until 1897*

A considerable number of 0–6–0 engines was obtained from Beyer, Peacock of both double and single framed varieties, all of the maker's standard designs. This old view shows No 274, built in 1872, in its original condition

273 Class Double-framed Goods 0–6–0

Total in class at 1/1/23: 6. Built: Beyer, Peacock 1872–3

W. G. Beattie succeeded his father, Joseph Beattie, in October, 1871, at a time when several engines were under construction, some at Nine Elms and some at the works of outside contractors. The double-framed goods engines of the 273 Class, already ordered from the celebrated builder at Gorton, Manchester, were the first to appear, Nos 273–8 (Works Nos 1163–8) in June, 1872, and Nos 285–90 (Works Nos 1269–74) in June, 1873, total 12, of which six as detailed below, outlasted their original owners.

The principal dimensions of the six survivors, which had been rebuilt with new Adams boilers, were as follows: cylinders, 17in × 24in wheels, 5ft 1in diameter. The boiler, 4ft 4in × 9ft 7½in in the barrel, was pitched 6ft 5in above rail, pressed at 160lb, and contained 218 tubes, 1¾in diameter. Total hs, including firebox, 106·6sq ft, grate area 17·25sq ft. Power class was J.

The tender was a typical Beattie design with the coping prominently raked, and originally with handrail and footboard to allow the fireman to reach the tank-filler hole. It held 1,950 gallons and weighed 22 tons 15cwt in working order, which, added to the engine weight, 36 tons 9cwt, brought the total, wo, to 59 tons 4cwt. Over buffers, engine and tender measured 42ft 10½in.

The SR took over engines of this class as follows:

No	*Works No*	*Date*	*rebuilt**	*New No and Date*	*Wdn*
273	1163	6/72	4/93	0273 (2/98), 273A (1914)	12/24
274	1164	,,	7/93	0274 (2/98), 0229 (1914)	7/24
277	1167	,,	1/96	0277 (4/00), 277A (1914)	5/24
278	1168	,,	9/86	0278 (5/00), 278A (1914)	12/24
286	1270	6/73	11/86	0286 (2/00), 286A (1914)	12/24
288	1272	,,	8/94	0288 (2/00), 288A (1914)	12/24

* with new Adams boiler *Wdn*—withdrawn

Of the remaining six engines, 0275/6 were broken up 1905, leaving ten which were all withdrawn 1913 and subsequently reinstated. Of these ten, No 285A was broken up 11/21, 287A 5/22, 289A 11/21 and 351A 12/21. No 351A was originally No 290, which came into the duplicate list as 0290 in 6/98, was restored to the 'capital' numeration as 351 in 12/99, replacing one of W. G. Beattie's '348' class 4-4-0s, was again duplicated as 0351 in 6/00, and later renumbered 351A.

No 273A was one of those withdrawn prior to World War I, but laid aside and subsequently re-instated owing to the war emergency. It is seen here shunting at Wimbledon in 1922

No 288A at the time of its resuscitation still sported a stovepipe chimney, this picture being taken at Guildford in 1920

No 286A after a still further overhaul and repaint, as it returned to Strawberry Hill in October, 1921

About 1897, members of this sturdy-looking class were noted at Salisbury and elsewhere with standard Adams number plates, and it is believed that new ones were cast for Nos 0273/4 when transferred to the duplicate list in 1898.

In their latest years, the surviving 273 Class engines were engaged on miscellaneous freight and ballast work, and Strawberry Hill depot could nearly always display one or more examples.

The SR withdrew all six surviving engines in 1924.

302 Class Inside-framed Goods 0-6-0

Total in class: 36. Built: Beyer, Peacock 1874-8

We now come to W. G. Beattie's first design of his own, a mainline goods engine of generous proportions, compared with which the 'Ilfracombe Goods' were diminutive. These engines, the 302 Class (or 'Class No 6' according to certain official records), were in some respects like the elder Beattie's 0–6–0 type, but with inside frames only. They were built by Beyer, Peacock in three lots of a dozen each and had boiler mountings of Beyer's usual style and finish, with polished chimney cap and dome, but the splashers were closed and had a single strip of brass edging without Beyer's customary works plate.

The principal dimensions were originally as follows: cylinders (inside) 17in × 22in. Wheel diameter 5ft 0in. Wheelbase, engine, 6ft 0in + 8ft 0in = 14ft 0in; tender, 10ft 3in equally spaced; total (E & T.) 31ft 4½in. Length over buffers 41ft 10¼in. The boiler barrel, 4ft 0in external diameter by 9ft 3½in long, contained 229 1·9/16in diameter tubes, giving a heating surface of 893sq ft, to which the firebox added 132sq ft, total hs 1,025sq ft. The working pressure was 120lb per sq in, which at the time was the standard figure. The firebox was 5ft 1in long outside and was raised; at its left-hand side was the customary Beattie steam feed pump. The grate area was 15·5sq ft. The tender ran on six wheels, 3ft 9¾in in diameter, carried 1,950 gallons, and weighed (full) 20 tons 15cwt, which added to the engine weight (wo) of 34 tons 2cwt, brought the total to 54 tons 17cwt. Power class—K (except No. 0152 which was J).

As was usual with the elder Beattie's engines, this class also bore plates on the cab sides recording 'Beattie's Patent', and indicating that the various features of Joseph Beattie's régime, such as feed-water heater, etc, were incorporated and enjoyed the right of royalty payment from the railway company.

The dimensions of the '302' class, as rebuilt by Adams with standard boilers, were as follows: wheel diameter, 5ft 1in (indicating thicker tyres), cylinders 17in × 24in, working pressure 160lb. The new boiler was 4ft 4in × 9ft 3½in in the barrel, pitched 7ft 0in above rail, and contained 218 1¾in tubes. Heating surface, tubes 952sq ft, firebox 111sq ft, total hs, 1,063sq ft, grate area 16·2sq ft.

This rebuild included, of course, an Adams chimney, and the substitution of the Drummond type chimney did not generally commence until the end of the century. With Drummond chimney, the '302' class measured 12ft 6in from chimney top to rail.

The first of the later design of single-framed Beyer, Peacock goods, No 151 Montrose *built in 1878. It lasted until 1924, but had long since lost its name*

No 344 as rebuilt by Adams

Being mainly employed on yard shunting in their last year, pictures of Beattie's 0–6–0s out on the main line were not very easy to obtain, but this shows No 0369 running through Woking station on a local freight in 1924. Note that it had acquired an old tender from 2–4–0 No 120A Hecla

No	*wks No**	*date*	*reb*	*dupd*	*wdn*	*No*	*wks No**	*date*	*reb*	*dupd*	*wdn*
151	1777	4/78	—	1902	1924	336	1600	7/76	1889	1901	1922
152	1778	,,	1891	,,	,,	337	1601	,,	1893	,,	1924
160	1787	6/78	1890	1900	,,	338	1602	,,	1892	,,	,,
162	1788	,,	1886	,,	,,	339	1603	,,	—	—	1891
229	1779	4/78	,,	—	1925	340	1604	,,	1889	1901	1906
230	1780	,,	—	—	1889	341	1605	,,	1893	,,	1924
302	1360	6/74	1886	1900	1922	342	1606	,,	1894	,,	,,
303	1361	,,	,,	,,	,,	343	1607	,,	1891	,,	,,
304	1362	,,	1892	,,	1906	344	1608	,,	,,	,,	1921
305	1363	,,	1886	,,	1915	345	1609	,,	,,	1902	1925
306	1364	,,	1887	—	1892	346	1610	,,	—	—	1893
307	1365	,,	1886	1901	1915	347	1611	,,	1893	1901	1925
308	1366	,,	—	—	1892	368	1781	4/78	—	—	1893
309	1367	,,	1886	—	1890	369	1782	,,	1888	1901	1925
310	1368	,,	1893	1901	1915	370	1783	,,	1890	,,	1924
311	1369	,,	1886	,,	1925	371	1784	,,	1889	,,	1922
312	1370	,,	1894	,,	1894	,,	1785	5/78	1892	,,	1906
313	1371	,,	1887	,,	1914	373	1786	,,	—	,,	1903

* Beyer, Peacock *dupd*—relegated to duplicate list *reb*—rebuilt *wdn*—withdrawn

ENGINE SUMMARY

Nos 151, 152, 160, 162 were originally named, respectively, *Montrose*, *Marmion*, *Thames*, *Severn*.

The following were reinstated during World War I and renumbered as follows at the dates bracketed: **0160** to **160A** (1916), **0162** to **162A** (1916), **0229** to **229A** (1916), **0337** to **337A** (1915), **0347** to **347A** (1916), **0370** to **370A** (1916). **229A** again became **0229** when the double-framed goods **No 0229** was withdrawn (see page 31).

Nos 306, 308, 309, 346, 368 were not duplicated, and after withdrawal of these engines the numbers affected remained blank until occupied by renumbered Drummond goods engines of the 700 Class in 1898.

No 229 was successively renumbered **0229,** (1894), **229A** (1915) and **0229** (1924).

On being relegated to the duplicate list, most of this class had the cypher 'O' prefixed to suit, and some were provided with new number-plate castings of the Adams type. Others had small plates, displaying the data of rebuild, affixed to the driving splashers. The plan of drawing a cancellation line through the existing numerals on the cab sides came into vogue in the spring of 1902, and may have been applied to No 345.

Of the 'Ilfracombe Goods', two were broken up in 1905, but the remaining six were eventually sold to Colonel Stephens for use on his light railways, three on the Shropshire & Montgomery, two on the Kent & East Sussex and the remaining one, No 0394, on the East Kent. This one was the most interesting, as it was still in its approximately original condition, with dome on firebox

282 Class Light Goods 0–6–0

Total in class: 8. Built: Beyer, Peacock 1873–1880

At the period covered by the introduction of the 273 Class freight engines, viz, 1872–3, the line from Barnstaple to Ilfracombe was in progress, and in view of the fact that it was legally due to be completed by April, 1873, W. G. Beattie took into stock three light 0–6–0 engines of Beyer, Peacock's standard design. In fact, the new line was not opened until July, 1874, by which time he had acquired two more engines of the type from the same source. The aggregate of eight comprised the above five, plus one more added by Beattie in 1875, and two more by Adams in 1880, and this class has always been known as the 'Ilfracombe Goods'.

These engines, like everything that came from from Beyer at this period, were very handsomely designed and originally had Beyer's elegant standard chimney with polished cap, and truly magnificent works' plates, which spanned the entire arc of each driving splasher. The leading splashers were rimmed with brass beading, but those of the trailing wheels were screened by rectangular side sheets, or 'fenders', on which was mounted a small cab of the well-known Johnson pattern. The boiler was a 'straightback', and the dome with its spring balance safety valves, was placed over the firebox.

The 'Ilfracombe Goods' class had cylinders 16in × 20in, wheels 4ft 6in diameter, wheelbase (engine) 6ft 4in + 7ft 6in = 13ft 10in. The boiler was comparatively small, 3ft 8in × 9ft 3in in the barrel, pressed at 130lb and pitched only 6ft 1½in above rail. Adams rebuilt the first six engines with domed boilers, 4ft 0in diameter, pressed at 160lb, pitched 6ft 6in, and containing 182 1¾in tubes, against 150 2in tubes in the original type. The new boiler had 12·6sq ft of grate, against the 14sq ft reported as the original figure. The result of this rebuild was to increase the engine weight (in working order) from 25 tons 16cwt, to 26 tons 12cwt.

The reconstruction included the Adams standard cab, suitably adapted, and the replacement of the original four-wheeled tenders (weight full, only 13 tons 11¾cwt) by six-wheeled tenders of Beattie design. Other distinctive alterations were Adams' 'stove pipe' chimney and standard brass number-plates, displaying

The other 'Ilfracombe Goods' had been rebuilt and modified as shown in these two photographs. Shropshire & Montgomery No 6 'Thisbe' (formerly 0283), at Kinnerley in 1926. Kent & East Sussex No 9 Juno (formerly 0284) at Bodiam in 1931. These two engines lasted until 1937 and 1939 respectively

the date of rebuild. New plates were cast for this purpose as late as 3/99, when 282 became 0282, but when this engine was again renumbered (349) later in the same year, the numerals were painted on.

The maximum permissible load of an engine of this class on the heavy grades at Mortehoe (1 in 40 in the Down direction, 1 in 36 in the Up) was at first limited to 28 wheels.

No	*Works No**	*Date*	*Rebuilt*	*New No and Date*	*Disposal*
282	1208	2/73	6/89	0282 (1899) 349 (1899) 0349 (1900)	Sold
283	1209	,,	6/88	0283 (1899)	,,
284	1210	,,	,,	0284 (1899)	,,
300	1428	6/74	12/90	0300 (1900)	,,
301	1429	,,	5/90	0301 (1900)	Sc 12/05
324	1517	3/75	6/88	0324 (1900)	Sold

* Beyer, Peacock Sc—Scrapped

No	*Works No**	*Date*	*Rebuilt*	*New No and Date*	*Disposal*
393	2041	12/80	—	0393 (1902)	Sc 1/05
394	2042	,,	—	0394 (1902)	Sold

* Beyer, Peacock   Sc—Scrapped

DISPOSAL SUMMARY

0349 (282), sold 6/10 to Kent & East Sussex Railway, **No 7,** *Rother*, out of service by 1933.
0283, out of service (LSWR) 1/14, sold 5/16 to Shropshire & Montgomeryshire Railway, **No 6,** *Thisbe*, scrapped 1937.
0284, out of service (LSWR) 1/14, sold 11/14 to KESR, **No 9,** *Juno*, withdrawn 1939.
0300, out of service (LSWR) 1/14, sold 11/14 to SMR, **No 5,** *Pyramus*, scrapped 1932.
0324, out of service (LSWR) 8/10, sold 1/11 to SMR, **No 3,** *Hesperus*, scrapped 1941.
0394, out of service (LSWR) 1/14, sold 10/18 to East Kent Railway, **No 3,** scrapped 1932.
0301 and **0393** were the only engines of the class scrapped by LSWR.

As the table shows, the various light railways controlled by the late Col H. F. Stephens drew upon the 'Ilfracombe Goods' at second-hand for their motive power, and No 0394 went to the East Kent Railway largely in its original external condition. The principal differences comprised a six-wheel Beattie tender, Adams chimney, and Drummond 'lock-up' safety-valves instead of the original spring balances, but the dome was still over the firebox, and the 'two-piece' cab had not been superseded.

While in possession of the Shropshire & Montgomeryshire Railway, *Hesperus* was seen more than once at Crewe, probably for repair.

330 Class Shunting 0–6–0ST

Total in class: 20. Built: Beyer, Peacock 1876–82

In 1876, W. G. Beattie obtained from Beyer, Peacock six 0–6–0 saddle-tank engines of Beyer's standard type and these were found so suitable for heavy shunting duties, that others were obtained by Beattie and his successor during the next six years. The last twelve had Adams' 'stove pipe' chimney, overpainted dome casings and less of the brasswork detail that embellished the original lots, but were otherwise close counterparts.

The 'Saddlebacks', as these engines were nicknamed, were built with Salter spring-balance safety-valves mounted on the dome and loaded to 130lb per sq in, which remained the standard pressure for this class throughout its long and useful career. Only five were rebuilt with Drummond boilers, and these were at first pressed at 160lb, and afterwards at 150lb. Like all Drummond boilers, they had direct-loaded safety-valves mounted on the dome. They were not classed for power.

An interesting point about this class is that none of the engines ever had power brakes, but in this respect they were not unique among the South Western stock. A number of Western section (SR) shunting engines depended on hand brakes only, though they invariably had vacuum ejectors for purposes of train control. The few 'Saddlebacks' that were so fitted ultimately are detailed below.

The original dimensions were cylinders, 17in × 24in, wheel diameter 4ft 3in, wheelbase 13ft 9in. The boiler was pitched with its centre 6ft 4½in above rail,

Twenty 0–6–0STs for general yard shunting were ordered by W. G. Beattie from Beyer, Peacock to their own design. These were built between 1876 and 1882, and all lasted well into post-Grouping days. No 331 was one of the first engines built in 1876

No 0414 shunts in Nine Elms Yard in 1920

A few even survived to be rebuilt with Drummond type boilers, depicted by No 0333 at Eastleigh in 1927

and the barrel measured 4ft 0in maximum external diameter by 9ft 4in long, but details of the tubes, so far as number and diameter are concerned, have not been preserved. The total heating surface was 901sq ft, made up from 824sq ft tubular, and 77sq ft in the firebox. The grate area was 14sq ft, capacity of saddle-tank 800 gallons, and weight of engine in working order 34 tons 19cwt 2qtr.

Although officially withdrawn, the last engine of the class, No 0334 was kept intact in Eastleigh paintshop for some years and there it had as companions the ex-IWR 2–4–0T *Ryde*, built 1864, and Drummond's 4–2–4T inspection 'Cab'. The old saddle-tank was still in existence in 1948 on the scrap road outside Eastleigh Works. No 0335 also lasted until 1948 as KESR No 4. It had been exchanged for the 0–8–0T *Hecate* which became SR 949.

No	*Works No**	*Date*	*New No and Date*	*Wdn*	*No*	*Works No**	*Date*	*New No and Date*	*Wdn*
127	2125	5/82	0127 1911	1925§	332	1593	5/76	0332 1905	1933
128	2126	,,	0128 1911	1931	333	1594	,,	0333 1905	1929
131	2127	,,	0131 1911	1924	334	1595	,,	0334 1905	1933‡
149	2128	,,	0149 1902	1930	335	1596	,,	0335 1907	1932§
150	2129	,,	0150 1902	1929	409	2131	5/82	0409 1906	1924
161	2130	,,	0161 1903	1926	410	2132	6/82	0410 1906	1930
227	1698	6/77	†	1930	411	2133	,,	0411 1906	1927
228	1699	,,	†	1929	412	2134	,,	0412 1906	1925
330	1591	5/76	0330 1905	1924	413	2135	,,	0413 1906	1931
331	1592	,,	0331 1905	1930	414	2136	,,	0414 1906	1924

* Beyer, Peacock *Wdn*—Withdrawn § Sold, see below ‡ See below
† For successive renumberings of this engine, see below.

ENGINE SUMMARY

No 127 was sold to East Kent Railway, 12/25, EKR **No 7,** cut up at Ashford (SR), 3/46.

Nos 127, 128, 149, 316, 328, 331, to **335** and **412** were fitted with vacuum ejectors in their later years.

Nos 0128, 0149, 0331, 0332, 0333 had their original boilers replaced by Drummond boilers. The first three listed were rebuilt thus in 1924, the other two in 1923. At the same time they were fitted with Drummond chimneys, but this was not done with any of the rebuilt engines, which retains the Adams 'stove pipes' to the end.

No 227 was renumbered **0227** in 1894, **316** in 12/99, and **0316** in 1912.

No 228 was renumbered **0228** in 1894, **328** in 1899, and **0328** in 1911. For many years, this engine worked the passenger service between Clapham Junction and Kensington (Addison Road, now Olympia).

No 0334 stored at Eastleigh until 1938 when it was loaned to the East Kent Railway. The number 3334 was stencilled on the frames. Not cut up until April 1949.

No 0335 was transferred 7/32 to KESR (in exchange for *Hecate*, as noted in text), KESR **No 4,** and was cut up at Ashford 8/48.

NOTE—The engines renumbered after 1902 did not bear the cypher 'O', see Introduction. Those duplicated by a line drawn beneath the existing numerals, displayed the line in gold, to ensure its prominence on the dark green goods livery.

One of Joseph Beattie's earliest 2–4–0WTs in a class of three which emerged from Nine Elms works in 1858. No 143 Nelson *lasted until 1882. These were the forerunners of the better known engines introduced in 1863*

From 1863 on, Joseph Beattie built 85 2–4–0WTs for the London suburban services. The last came out under his son. No 33, Phoenix, *here in original condition, was built at Nine Elms in 1872, and withdrawn in 1890*

An early view of No 191, another of the original 1863 engines. This one lasted until 1896

The story of the Beattie 2–4–0WTs may now be skipped conveniently for the next 20 years, until 1920, when three were still at work at Wadebridge, Cornwall, having been found the only suitable engines for the Wenford Bridge mineral line. As a consequence, they had been retained and undergone various renewals and rebuildings. Between their normal duties they also undertook local passenger work; this view of No 0298 (still with an Adams boiler) was taken near Padstow in 1921

329 Class Suburban 2–4–0WT

Total in class at 1/1/23: 3. Built: Beyer, Peacock 1874–5

The deliveries of new engines from outside contractors in W. G. Beattie's early days as locomotive superintendent included 12 more of the celebrated 2–4–0 suburban well-tanks with Allan straight link motion, which Beyer, Peacock delivered in two lots of six each in 1874 and 1875.

The main distinction was that the 1875 engines had 6in longer frames and rectangular splashers of the kind already adopted on the few engines of the class that had been built at Nine Elms.

The surviving engines had been kept in service specially to work the china clay traffic on the lightly-laid branches to Wenford Bridge and Ruthern Bridge. No 3329 (old 329) retained the rectangular splashers above noted, and all three displayed, at their leading wheels, the characteristic Beattie 'floating' outside axleboxes, which are directly sprung from the lower slide-bars without guides, or any form of support other than the laminated controlling springs. These outside bearings are auxiliary to the main, and orthodox bearings on the inside frames, and were intended purely to check the rolling tendency liable to arise from the combination of outside cylinders and an extremely compact wheelbase.

The three engines in question were extensively rebuilt at various periods. The first scheme, carried out between 1884 and 1892, comprised Adams boiler, cab and chimney. The second, carried out 19[illegible]–2, comprised Drummond boiler, but nothing radical beyond this, and the third and last 1931–5, comprised new cylinders, Drummond chimney, and a new portion of frame at the front end, with a new steel buffer beam to suit.

The principal dimensions of these surviving engines were as follows: Outside cylinders, 16½in × 20in. Wheel diameter, coupled 5ft 7in (5ft 6in original), leading 3ft 7¾in (originally 3ft 6in). Wheelbase, 5ft 6in + 7ft 0in, total 12ft 6in. Front overhang, 6ft 11½in, rear ditto, 6ft 8½in, over buffers 26ft 2in. The boiler, 4ft 2in × 8ft 10½in barrel, is pitched 6ft 6½in above rail, pressed at 160lb, and contains 179 1¾in diameter tubes giving 753sq ft heating surface, to which the firebox adds 94sq ft, total hs 847·0sq ft. The outside firebox is 4ft 10½in long,

In 1921/2 all three surviving engines received Drummond boilers with pop safety valves on the dome, although retaining for the time being their Adams stovepipe chimneys. No 0314 at Wadebridge in 1922 still carried the donkey pump on the left hand side of the firebox

No 0329 (here as Southern 3329) differed from the other two survivors in having rectangular splashers

and the grate area 14·8sq ft. The two wells, one immediately under the boiler barrel, and the other beneath the bunker, have a combined capacity of 550 gallons. Weight of engine in working order, 11 tons 3cwt + 13 tons 3cwt + 13 tons 10cwt, total 37 tons 16cwt.

Listed below is the complete delivery of 12 engines in which the ultimate three units were comprised. They were all built with Beattie's patent feed-water heater, and as late as 1922 No 314 was noted at Wadebridge with Beattie's steam feed pump on the left-hand side of the firebox.

No	*Works No**	*Date*	*Rt*	*Wdn*	*No*	*Works No**	*Date*	*Rt*	*Wdn*
34	1411	6/74	—	7/95	44	1533	11/75	12/87	11/98
201	1409	5/74	—	12/88†	325	1534	10/75	—	12/88†
202	1410	,,	—	7/98	326	1535	,,	—	Sold
					327	1536	,,	—	11/92†
298	1412	,,	6/84 11/21 5/33	1962	328	1537	,,	—	9/98
299	1413	,,	—	12/89†	329	1538	,,	12/92 4/22 9/35	1962
314	1414	,,	5/89 8/21 6/31	1962					

* B.P. † Date scrapped *Rt*—Rebuilt *Wdn*—Withdrawn

ENGINE SUMMARY

No 34 was originally named *Osprey*, and **No 44** *Pluto* till rebuilt, when Adams removed the name and substituted brass numerals.

No 202 became **0202** in 8/91.

Nos 298, 314, 329 were relegated to duplicate list and renumbered **0298, 0314, 0329** respectively in 6/98, 7/01, 10/01 and were renumbered in the SR 3000 Series (becoming **3298,** etc.,) under the 1931 scheme.

They became respectively **Nos 30587, 30585,** and **30586** on being taken over by British Railways, and ran until December 1962, with a length of service three times that of any of their sisters. **No 30586** was cut up in March 1964, but the other two have been preserved.

An historic occasion, and the final chapter, in the story of the Beattie 2-4-0WTs, resulted from the activities of the Stephenson Locomotive and Railway Correspondence & Travel societies. 30585 and 30587 were brought back to London, where they had not been seen for over 60 years, to work a special tour over some LSWR suburban routes, including the Hampton Court and Shepperton branches. Here they leave Surbiton, December 1962

The first 4–4–0s on the LSWR were of W. G. Beattie's design, 20 being built by Sharp, Stewart in 1877, Nos 348–367. They were very unsatisfactory machines and in spite of rebuilding by Adams, nearly all of them went to the scrap heap in the 1890s. This view shows 362 as built

348 Class Express 4–4–0

Total in class: 20. Built: Sharp, Stewart 1876–7

At the end of 1876, a mild sensation was caused on the LSWR by the appearance of a bogie express engine, which had been built to W. G. Beattie's designs by Sharp, Stewart, whose works were then at Manchester. At this time, not many railways had adopted bogie engines for express work, and the LSWR ranked among the first users of the type in the south of England.

The first engine of this pioneer design, No 348, was a remarkable advance on any existing South Western class, and was in many respects unique, both in its details and its appearance. A striking external feature was the single long box splasher covering both coupled wheels, and somewhat resembling a side tank. The cab had a Stirling touch, and taken altogether, these engines, with their 'stove-pipe' chimneys, bore a certain resemblance to later Adams designs—clearly a foretaste of future developments.

The 348 Class engines were the last to be fitted with Beattie's patent firebox, and a novel feature was the use of piston valves. Unfortunately, these had no means of water relief, and damage was constantly occurring through water trapped in the steam chests and cylinders.

When new, this class was nominally the most powerful in the south, and worked the fast expresses between London, Southampton, Portsmouth and Exeter, but, taken as a whole, they were somewhat of a failure, principally because their boilers were undersized for the 18½in cylinders when the demand for steam was heavy. The cylinders were afterwards lined to a 17½in bore, but it is not known whether Beattie had this done, and in any case Adams took most of the class off the express links, and relegated them to lighter duties, principally between Southampton and Weymouth. For this purpose they were allocated to Dorchester and to the old depot at Northam, but in the early 1890s, some were confined to the Exeter–Plymouth expresses, over the very hard road which crosses Dartmoor, having gradients as steep as 1 in 58, 1 in 70 and 1 in 80.

Eight of these engines were rebuilt and externally modified by Adams with a more orthodox type of splasher, made in one with the sandbox, and a cab of the Adams type which greatly improved the comforts of the footplate. The 'up and down' running plate was straightened at the same time, and the appearance generally was smartened up, but the frames were too light to stand up to their new burdens for very long, and since the performance was not remarkably improved, the rebuilding scheme was not prosecuted further. The principal dimensions, before and after the above conversion, were as follows.

	New	*Rebuilt*
Cylinders	18½in × 26in	17in × 26in
Wheels, bogie	3ft 3in	3ft 3in
,, coupled	6ft 7in	6ft 7in
Wheelbase, engine... ...	22ft 6in*	22ft 6in*
,, tender ...	10ft 3in	13ft 0in
,, E. & T. ...	40ft 1in	43ft 4in
Boiler barrel	4ft 2in × 10ft 4in	4ft 4in × 11ft 0in
,, pitch	7ft 0in	7ft 4in
,, pressure	140lb	160lb
Tubes	218 × 1¾in	216 × 1⅝in
Heating surface (*sq ft*):		
Tubes	889·64	1,121
Firebox	145·7	110
Total	1,035·34	1,231
Grate area (*sq ft*)	17·86	17
Weight (*engine, wo*) ...	43 tons 16cwt	44 tons 6cwt
Tender capacity (*gallons*)	2,250	3,000
Over buffers (*E and T*) ...	47ft 4¾in	51ft 4¾in

* Divided: 6ft 6in + 7ft 0in + 9ft 0in

There was a total of 20 engines built, and subsequent historians like Ahrons considered that the outcome would have been more satisfactory if Beattie had

Beattie 4–4–0 No 351 as rebuilt by Adams, at Exmouth in 1892

thoroughly tried out the prototype engine before embarking on such extensive construction of a totally new type. The engines were numbered 348 to 367, Works' Nos (SSC) 2657 to 2676. No 348 was dated 1876 and the others, 1877.

No	*Rt*	*New No and Date*	*Sc or *Wdn*	*No*	*Rt*	*New No and Date*	*Sc or*
348	1888	0348 1900	*1905	357	1889	0357 1900	*1905
349	1889	—	3/99	358	—	—	12/93
350	1889	—	12/89	359	—	—	4/90
351	1889	—	11/99	360	—	—	12/93
352	—	—	12/89	361	—	—	3/94
353	1890	0353 1900	*1905	362	—	—	10/92
				363	—	—	3/94
354	1889	0354 1900	*1905	364	—	—	11/94
355	,,	—	12/90	365	—	0365 1896	10/98
356	,,	0356 1900	*1905	366	—	—	3/94
				367	—	—	9/91

* Date withdrawn; the other dates in this column are those of scrapping.
Rt—Rebuilt *Sc*—Scrapped *Wdn*—Withdrawn

318 Class Metropolitan Bogie 4–4–0T

Total in class: 6. Built: Beyer, Peacock 1875

These engines were the first bogie tanks used by the LSWR, and were intended for fast passenger trains between Exeter and Plymouth. Nicknamed 'Plymouth tanks' as a result, they were a Beyer design similar to engines already supplied by that firm to the Metropolitan, the District and other companies for working traffic over the underground systems.

The genesis of this celebrated design is traced to an experimental 4–4–0T which J. C. Craven built at Brighton in 1859 for working the LBSC branch from Crystal Palace to its temporary terminus at Battersea pending completion of Victoria station. This particular engine, LBSC No 136, was not a pronounced success, but the design when improved on by Beyer's had a tremendous vogue, both in this country and on the Continent.

Between 1862 and 1886, about 148 engines of the type were supplied to various English companies, of which the Metropolitan was the largest user with 72 units. Next came the Metropolitan District with 54, followed by the LNW with 16, and the Midland and the LSWR with six each.

The six with which we are concerned here differed in details from the original Beyer design, though the dimensions were the same. The LSWR engines were non-condensing, and had Ramsbottom type safety-valves over the firebox, whereas the other engines mentioned had spring balances mounted on the dome. Also, the LSWR lot was equipped with Beattie's patent feed-water heating apparatus, the steam pump for which was placed in front of the left-hand tank, and the legend, 'Beattie's Patent' was incorporated in the rectangular works plates on the tank sides.

The leading dimensions of these engines were as follows. Outside cylinders 17in × 24in. Wheel diameter, bogie 3ft, coupled 5ft 9in. Wheelbase, coupled 8ft 7in, total 20ft 6in. Working pressure, 120lb per sq in. The boiler barrel

No 318 as built, and . . .

measured 4ft 0in × 10ft $0\frac{1}{2}$in, and contained 212 $1\frac{9}{16}$in. tubes, giving 896sq ft of heating surface, to which the firebox added 96sq ft, total hs 992sq ft. The grate area was 17·4sq ft, tank capacity 1,100 gallons, coal space 53 cubic ft (approximately 1 ton 17cwt), weight of engine in working order, 44 tons 2cwt.

The coal space was covered over by the cab roof, which extended to the back plate of the bunker, and coaling had to be done from the footplate—an inconvenient and uncleanly method that made the engines very unpopular.

In Adams' days, all the shapely Beyer chimneys with copper caps were replaced by the standard 'stove pipes', and one engine No 318, had its original bogie (which was of the Bissell type) replaced by an Adams bogie of longer wheelbase with spring-controlled side-play.

These engines did very little work on the Plymouth road, and were soon transferred to the London end and rostered to the Leatherhead services, for which purpose two were stationed in the LSWR shed there. In the middle 'nineties No 323 was often in evidence between Weymouth and Bournemouth, and by the early years of the present century most of them had been relegated to various branches in the New Forest district. All six had their numbers prefixed by cypher 'O' in 1900 to suit the range of Drummond 0–4–4 M7 tanks produced in that year, and none was rebuilt.

No	*Works No (BP)*	*Date*	*Scrapped*
318	1354	1875	1906
319	1355	,,	1909
320	1356	,,	1913
321	1357	,,	1907
322	1358	,,	1908
323	1359	,,	1906

. . . No 320 as subsequently modified by Adams

CHAPTER FOUR

THE ADAMS ENGINES

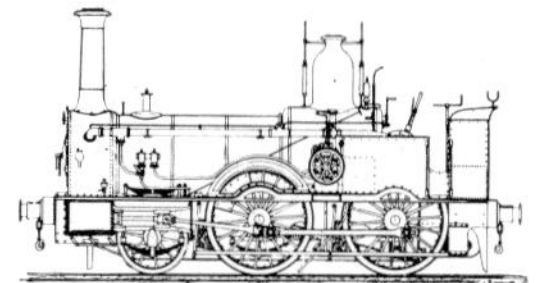

46 Class Bogie 4–4–0T

Total in class: 12. Built: Beyer, Peacock 1879

ADAMS' first design, on succeeding to the position vacated through ill-health by W. G. Beattie in 1877, was a suburban passenger tank engine of the 4–4–0 type with disc bogie wheels and a general appearance of solidity which earned the class the nickname of 'Ironclads', though earlier accounts sometimes referred to them as 'Steamrollers'.

The principal dimensions were as follows. Outside cylinders, 18in × 24in. Wheel diameter, bogie 2ft 6in, coupled, 5ft 7in. Wheelbase, coupled 8ft 6in, total 21ft 8½in. The boiler worked at 140lb, was pitched with its centre line 7ft 0in above rail, and measured 4ft 2in × 10ft 0¾in in the barrel. Heating surface, 199 1¾in tubes, 947sq ft; firebox 100sq ft, total hs 1,047sq ft. The firebox was 5ft 8in long outside and the grate area 16sq ft. Height over chimney 13ft 2¾in, weight in working order 52 tons. They were built by Beyer, Peacock (Nos 1832–1843 of 1879).

These engines were fitted with Church's patent steam valves, for which Beyer's held the rights, and were so recorded on a small oblong plate fixed to the angle iron above the cylinders. These were apparently circular valves which were liable to stick when 'dry' of steam (e.g., after a long wait at a station) and are said to have been hideously 'screechy' at the moment of re-starting. They were also difficult to keep steam-tight as might be expected in view of the foregoing.

Between 1883 and 1886, the whole class was converted to the 4–4–2 wheel arrangement by the addition of a pair of radial trailing wheels, 3ft 0in diameter, which increased the total wheelbase to 28ft 5½in, the length over buffers to 36ft 5½in, and the weight (wo) to 58 tons 19cwt, of which 33 tons 15cwt were on the coupled wheels. The extended bunker provided 84 cubic feet of coal space, equivalent capacity 3 tons, and allowed a well to be fitted underneath which increased the total water capacity to 1,650 gallons.

After conversion, these engines were not again altered to any great extent, although most of them in due course received Drummond chimneys and had the cut-out brass numerals replaced by the customary transfers. It is curious that these engines did not display the Company's initials on the tank sides, and were, in fact, the only side-tank engines of Adams' design distinguished by this absence. Replaced, when the time came, by Drummond M7 0–4–4 tanks, they nevertheless contrived to last for over 20 years on the duplicate list, and several finally migrated to Hamworthy Junction, where they won a fresh nickname—'Hamworthy Buses'.

Adams first design for the LSWR was a series of 4–4–0Ts for suburban work in the London area, built by Beyer, Peacock in 1879. No 379 in original condition

Enlarged bunkers and trailing wheels were soon provided, converting them to 4–4–2Ts. No 377 is in this form

Apart from the provision of Drummond chimneys they remained almost unaltered. The last survivor was 0375, here at Bournemouth in 1925

No 0376 was sold in 1914, later became Brecon & Merthyr Railway No 44, and was absorbed into GWR stock in 1922, allocated GWR No 1391 (but never actually carried). As such, this engine was withdrawn in September of that year. It will be noted from the table that nine were taken over by the SR as working engines, and of these No 375 was the last actually in traffic. Most of the others had lain derelict in Eastleigh yard for several years. Also interesting is the fact that the first one built, No 46, was the last one relegated to the LSWR duplicate list.

No	*Rt*	*New No and Date*	*Wdn*	*No*	*Rt*	*New date and Date*	*Wdn*
46	4/86	046/1905	1/25	374	9/86	0374/1903	12/24
123	1/86	0123/1903	11/21	375	10/84	0375/1903	10/25
124	3/83	0124/1903	11/21	376	12/83	0376/1903	2/14 (*Sold*)
130	6/85	0130/1903	5/24	377	7/86	0377/1903	12/24
132	11/85	0132/1903	12/24	378	8/85	0378/1903	12/24
133	1/85	0133/1903	11/21	379	11/84	0379/1903	11/21

Rt—Rebuilt from 4-4-0T to 4-4-2T. *Wdn*—Withdrawn.

415 Class Passenger 4–4–2T

Total in Class: 71. Built: Stephenson; Beyer, Peacock; Neilson, and Dübs, 1882-1885

These engines were a natural development of the earlier 46 Class just described, the conversion of which to the 4–4–2T wheel arrangement commenced in 1883, just after the first twelve of the new engines had appeared the previous year, the rebuildings continuing contemporaneously with further examples of the new design. Of power Class K, they were built as follows:

1882 (September—November), 415–26, Beyer, Peacock & Co. (2167–78) ... 12
1883 427–8 (March), 429 (April), 430–1 (June), 432, 45/7–8 (October), 49–53 (November), 54–7 (December), Robt. Stephenson & Co. (2501–18) ... 18
1884 (November—December), 169–171/3, 490–5, Dübs & Co. (2000–9) 10
1885 (February—March) 479–89, Neilson & Co. (3200–10) 11
(June—October) 68, 77–8, 82, 104/6/7/25/6/9, Robt. Stephenson & Co. (2601–10) 10
(November—December) 516–25, Dübs & Co. (2105–14) 10

71

The principal dimensions of class 415 were:

Outside cylinders 17½in × 24in; coupled wheels 5ft 7in, carrying wheels 3ft 0in. Total wheelbase 29ft 5in, length over buffers 38ft 8¼in. Boiler 4ft 2in × 10ft 0in pitched at 7ft 0in above rail; firebox 6ft 2in long outside; total heating surface 1,059sq ft. Grate area 18·14sq ft. Working pressure 140lb, later 160lb per sq in. Weight in working order 54 tons 2cwt.

The twelve engines built by Beyer, Peacock in 1882, and the eighteen by Stephenson in the following year carried 1,000 gallons of water, but in subsequent lots the capacity of the tanks was increased to 1,200 gallons. The 20 engines

The previous class was developed into a numerous series of engines of the same wheel arrangement, but with well tanks in lieu of side tanks, 71 being built by outside firms between 1883 and 1885. Although nominally all of one class, later known as 0415, there were two distinct varieties. The first relied entirely on well tanks for water supply, and this view shows No 420 in its original condition

No 422 at Clapham Junction in 1922, with Drummond Chimney but otherwise practically unaltered

The later engines had slightly increased capacity, as a short side tank was embodied in the rear rectangular driving wheel splasher. No 518 in original condition

Two of the class received Drummond boilers in 1907, and No 0486 is seen here at Clapham Junction in 1920 making a quick movement after taking some vans over to the LBSC siding and returning to its own side of the station. This snappy operation involved crossing all four main lines of the LSWR, seldom all free at once

No 0517, one of the few to be repainted in SR colours, on a motor train at Guildford in 1925

By 1928 the remaining two were retained for working the Lyme Regis branch, with it sharp curves. A third engine came in 1946. Sold to the East Kent Railway in 1917, it was re-acquired by the SR under its equivalent old number, 3488 (prefix '3' replaced '0' after 1931). Under nationalisation the trio became 30582–30584, and this view shows No 30584 at Axminster in 1954

built 1885 by Stephenson and Dübs (10 each) had trailing wheels 3ft 6in diameter, 6in larger than those of the earlier engines.

No	*Wdn*	*No*	*Wdn*	*No*	*Wdn*	*No*	*Wdn*	*No*	*Wdn*	*No*	*Wdn*	*No*	*Wdn*
45	1924	57	1924	106	1924	417	1923	428	1925	485	1924	495	1922
47	1923	68 }	1925	107	1922	418	1922	429	1925	486	1928	516	1924
48	1921	58 }		125	1961	419	1923	430	1923	487	1924	517	1927
49	1921			126	1924	420	1923	431	1925	488	1961	518	1923
50	1927	77 }	1925	129	1924	421	1922	432	1922	489	1922	519	1926
51	1923	59 }		169	1926	422	1925	479	1921	490	1926	520	1961
52	1923			170	1923	423	1922	480	1925	491	1922	521	1925
53	1923	78 }	1922	171	1921	424	Sold	481	1924	492	1922	522	1928
54	1927	60 }		173	1923	425	1922	482	1923	493	1923	523	1923
55	1924	82	1922	415	1922	426	1924	483	1925	494	1922	524	1925
56	1922	104	1922	416	1925	427	1923	484	1922			525	1923

Two engines of this class were retained in service, **Nos 125** and **520,** SR **Nos 3125** and **3520** (duplicate list), to work the Lyme Regis branch. They had new frames and the bogies were allowed extra side play to suit the many sharp curves. In 1946 they were joined by 3488 (see below). They lasted well into BR days, becoming 30582 (3125), 30583 (3488), and 30584 (3520).

No 68 renumbered **58,** 1889; **No. 77** renumbered **59,** 1890; **No 78** renumbered **60,** 1890.

No 0479 was the first engine of this class to be scrapped.

The following engines were reboilered with boilers of the original design: **57** (4/95), **170** (6/98), **483** (5/95), **486** (12/97), **490** (6/98), **492** (11/95).

The following were reboilered with boilers of Drummond's design in which direct loaded safety-valves are mounted on the dome: **125** (SR **3125**) (1941), **486** (1907), **520** (1907).

424 sold to Government, 7/16.

480, 481, 485, 487 were lent to the Highland Railway, 2/18. The first two were returned to the LSWR 1919, and the other two in 1921.

488 was sold to the Government's Ridham General Salvage Depot, Sittingbourne, Kent, 9/17. Resold to East Kent Railway, 1919, EKR No. **5.** Resold to SR 1946 and became SR **No 3488,** withdrawn in 1961 and purchased by the Bluebell Railway.

In LSWR days, the Company's initials did not appear on the above class.

Transfer of '415' class locos. to duplicate list began in 1904, when the cypher 'O' was prefixed to each number affected. The complete list of transfers is as follows:

1904: Nos 169, 170, 171, 173, 415–429; **1905:** Nos 45, 47–55, 104, 106, 107, 430, 431, 432. **1906:** Nos 56, 57, 58, 59, 60. **1908:** No 82. **1911:** Nos 125, 126, 129, 479, 480, 481. **1914:** Nos 482–491. **1921:** Nos 517, 519, 520. **1922:** No 522. **1924:** Nos 521, 524. Nos 492–495, 516, 518, 523, and 525 never actually carried duplicate numbers.

The withdrawal dates are when the engines were officially taken out of stock, but many of them had lain derelict in Eastleigh yard for several years.

Nearly all of the class eventually received Drummond chimneys, but Nos 051, 052, 057, 492, and 516 retained the Adams stove pipes until scrapped; No 0428 until at least 1920.

Between 1913 and 1923 Nos 045, 050, 052, 054, 058, 0106, 0129, 0416, 0422, 0426, 0485, 0486, 517, 520, and 524 were fitted with pull and push apparatus on the old pulley and trolley system for branch line work.

T1 & F6 Classes Passenger 0–4–4T

Total in classes: 50. Built: L.S.W.R. 1888–96

In June, 1888, the first engine of an entirely new South Western class appeared from Nine Elms Works, a 0–4–4 bogie passenger tank, which was really a tank engine version of the A12 or 'Jubilee' 0–4–2s. The new class comprised 20 engines, Class T1, Nos 61–80, and, except in one particular noted below, the

T1 class No 3 in original condition

various data, relevant to the A12 cylinders and boiler apply and need not be repeated. The exceptional dimension was the 7ft 3½in boiler pitch, Class T1, against the 7ft 6in pitch, Class A12, a reduction of 2½in exactly corresponding to the smaller diameter of the T1 coupled wheels, which measured 5ft 7in against the A12 diameter of 6ft 0in.

The other T1 dimensions demanding record were: Bogie wheels, 3ft 0in diameter; wheelbase, 8ft 0in + 10ft 0in + 5ft 0in, total 23ft 0in. Tank capacity, 1,200 gallons, weight in working order, 53 tons, distributed as detailed in the subjoined comparison.

The T1 tanks of this first lot had the steam chest underneath the cylinders in the same manner as the first lot of A12s, but later examples were built with the steam chest between, and this alteration was made as well in the later lots of A12s. The second T1 lot, comprising 30 engines built at Nine Elms 1894–6, and thereby covering the transition from Adams to Drummond, was originally Classed F6, and differed from the earlier design principally in the steam-chest layout mentioned, and in weight. There was also a small increase in firebox heating surface (111sq ft against 110sq ft) and grate area (17·85sq ft against 17sq ft). The weight of the two lots of engines compared as follows:

	T1	*F6*
On leading wheels ...	17 tons 3cwt	16 tons 6cwt
On driving wheels ...	18 tons 0cwt	18 tons 6cwt
On trailing bogie ...	17 tons 17cwt	20 tons 10cwt
Total (wo) ...	53 tons 0cwt	55 tons 2cwt

from which it is evident that the new lot had 11cwt less available for adhesion, though the total engine weight was increased by over 2 tons.

The last 10 engines of Class F6 were ordered by Adams, but he had retired to his Putney retreat before they were finished, and they appeared with Drummond's number plates, Adams chimneys and minus brass beading.

The two classes here reviewed were intended for the London suburban services, and were constantly in evidence at all the compass points of the region concerned, including Ludgate Hill. Although not so common in the West of England as the later and smaller O2 0–4–4Ts, a few T1s and F6s were always to be found at its various outposts. Plymouth and Fratton depots were rarely, if ever, without any, and such widely-scattered places as Andover, Bournemouth,

Eastleigh and Salisbury regularly had an allocation and they worked such branches as Sidmouth and Swanage for many years.

They were fitted with steam brake and vacuum ejector, and included in power Class K.

Drummond chimneys first appeared on these 0–4–4T engines early in the 1900s. T1s Nos 71 and 78 were the first two concerned but not all the Adams chimneys had been replaced when the SR took over the engines. The last ones to retain stove pipes were No 1 (until 1920), 2 (1922), 8 (1923), 12 (1922), 16 (1925), 17 (1928), 18 (1923), 19 (1931), 20 (1926), 358 (1919), 359 (1925), 362 (1924), 363 (1927) 365 (1917), and 367 (1923).

No	*Order No*	*Date*	*Nine Elms Works No*	*Wdn*	*No*	*Order No*	*Date*	*Nine Elms Works No*	*Wdn*
61	T.1–1	6/88	259	1932	6	F.6–6	6/94	420	1947
62	T.1–2	12/88	265	1933	7	F.6–7	7/94	421	1951
63	T.1–3	"	266	"	8	F.6–8	8/94	422	1949
64	T.1–4	"	267	1932	9	F.6–9	"	424	1948
65	T.1–5	"	268	1934	10	F.6–10	"	425	1948
66	T.1–6	"	269	1932	11	S.6–1	6/95	454	1944
67	T.1–7	"	270	1931	12	S.6–2	"	455	1933
68	T.1–8	3/89	271	"	13	S.6–3	"	456	1949
69	T.1–9	"	272	"	14	S.6–4	"	457	1933
70	T.1–10	4/89	273	1934	15	S.6–5	7/95	458	1944
71	D.2–1	6/89	274	1936	16	S.6–6	8/95	459	1946
72	D.2–2	"	275	1933	17	S.6–7	9/95	461	1945
73	D.2–3	10/89	279	1936	18	S.6–8	"	462	1935
74	D.2–4	"	280	1934	19	S.6–9	11/95	464	1937
75	D.2–5	12/89	289	1935	20	S.6–10	"	465	1951
76	D.2–6	4/90	293	1933	358	A.7–1	6/96	484	1944
77	D.2–7	6/90	297	1932	359	A.7–2	"	485	1943
78	D.2–8	8/90	302	1933	360	A.7–3	"	486	1944
79	D.2–9	9/90	303	"	361	A.7–4	"	487	1949
80	D.2–10	"	304	1936	362	A.7–5	7/96	488	1939
1	F.6–1	4/94	413	1949	363	A.7–6	"	489	1948
2	F.6–2	5/94	415	1949	364	A.7–7	"	490	1944
3	F.6–3	"	416	1948	365	A.7–8	8/96	491	1938
4	F.6–4	6/94	417	"	366	A.7–9	"	492	1948
5	F.6–5	"	418	1950	367	A.7–10	"	493	1951

No 63, fitted with Drummond boiler, at Havant in 1927

In later days the T1s were chiefly used on branch lines, many fitted for working pull and push trains. No 367 at Virginia Water in 1926

No 1 (here at Eastleigh in 1945) was one of the dozen or so to survive Nationalisation in 1948, but they only lasted a year or two longer, and none was renumbered into the 30000s

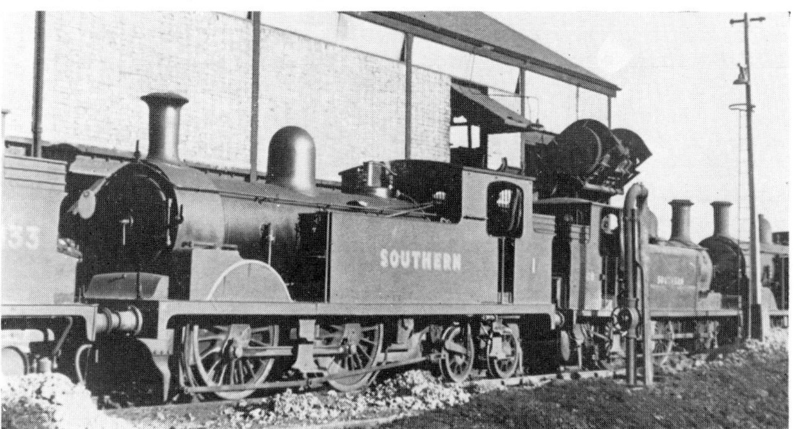

ENGINE SUMMARY

Nos 1 to **6** were lent to LMSR for the Somerset & Dorset line, 1941. **No 3** was returned to SR 6/1/45, the other five returned 10/3/45. **Nos 1** and **2** were stationed at Highbridge, and **Nos 3** to **6** at Templecombe.

The following were at one time adapted for pull-and-push working on the old cable and pulley system: **Nos 1, 4, 5, 8, 18, 359, 361, 367.**

Nos 7 and **364** were withdrawn respectively 2/39 and 3/39, and both were reinstated 10/39 to meet wartime engine demands.

The following received Drummond boilers at the dates bracketed: **Nos 11** (1935), **15** (1939), **63** (1926), **361** (1941). **No 11** reverted to Adams boiler in 1938, but the other three retained their's until scrapped.

Surviving engines in 1948 were allocated numbers 30001 etc, by BR in accordance with its renumbering scheme, but although a few lasted until 1951 none of them actually carried its new number.

Class O2 No 215 as originally built

O2 Class Passenger 0-4-4T

Total in class: 60. Built: LSWR. 1889–95

Following on the T1/F6 Class just described, came a smaller 0–4–4T built at Nine Elms to replace the Beattie well-tanks on branch line and short distance passenger work. These new engines, Class O2, were numbered 177 to 236, and are chiefly remembered for providing the bulk of the motive power used in the Isle of Wight during the SR period.

Seeing that the 'Islanders' all rejoiced in names honouring the various places served, it is interesting that No 185 of this class was the only Adams engine ever named by Adams (the Adams 0–4–0Ts, Class B4, allocated to Southampton Docks, were named by authority of the Docks Superintendent). The occasion was the opening of the branch line from Brookwood to Bisley Camp, July 12, 1890, when this engine, then quite new, conveyed H.R.H. the Princess of Wales (the future Queen Alexandra) to the first meet of the National Rifle Association. The name *Alexandra*, with the Prince of Wales' feathers underneath it, was painted on the side tanks to commemorate this event, and the engine worked thus until its next repaint, November, 1896.

The principal dimensions of Class O2 were as follows. Cylinders, Nos 177–196, 17in × 24in; Nos 197–236, $17\frac{1}{2}$in × 24in, which later applied throughout the class. Wheel diameter, coupled 4ft 10in, bogie 3ft 0in. Wheelbase, 6ft 10in + 8ft 6in + 5ft 0in, total 20ft 4in. The boiler, pressed at 160lb and pitched 6ft $10\frac{1}{2}$in above rail, contained 201 $1\frac{3}{4}$in tubes in a barrel measuring 4ft 2in minimum external diameter by 9ft 5in long. Heating surface: tubes, 897·75sq ft, firebox 89·75sq ft, total hs 987·50sq ft. The firebox was 5ft 0in long outside, grate area 13·83sq ft. Other dimensions were: Height over chimney, 13ft $2\frac{3}{4}$in length over buffers 30ft $8\frac{1}{2}$in, tank capacity 800 gallons. The weight in working order was originally quoted as 44 tons $11\frac{1}{2}$cwt, which appears to have been the 'mean weight', i.e., with tanks and bunker half full, as was the customary rating of the period. The later figure was 46 tons 18cwt total, distributed 15 tons 1cwt + 15 tons 9cwt + 16 tons 8cwt, but the engines in the Isle of Wight weight 2 tons heavier, as detailed opposite. Power class was K.

No	*Order No*	*Date*	*Nine Elms Works No*	*Wdn*	*No*	*Order No*	*Date*	*Nine Elms Works No*	*Wdn*
177	O.2–1	12/89	284	1959	207	D.4–1	12/91	338	1957
178	O.2–2	12/89	290	*	208	D.4–2	,,	339	*
179	O.2–3	3/90	291	1959	209	D.4–3	,,	341	*
180	O.2–4	4/90	292	*	210	D.4–4	,,	342	*
181	O.2–5	5/90	294	*	211	D.4–5	3/92	347	*
182	O.2–6	,,	295	1960	212	D.4–6	5/92	351	1959
183	O.2–7	,,	296	1961	213	D.4–7	,,	353	1953
184	O.2–8	6/90	298	*	214	D.4–8	6/92	354	1940
185	O.2–9	,,	299	1940	215	D.4–9	,,	355	*
186	O.2–10	7/90	301	*	216	D.4–10	,,	356	1957
187	B.3–1	10/90	305	1945	217	D.4–11	,,	357	*
188	B.3–2	,,	306	*	218	D.4–12	8/92	358	*
189	B.3–3	,,	307	1933	219	D.4–13	9/92	359	*
190	B.3–4	11/90	308	*	220	D.4–14	,,	360	*
191	B.3–5	,,	309	1933	221	D.4–15	,,	361	1953
192	B.3–6	,,	310	1961	222	D.4–16	,,	362	1933
193	B.3–7	,,	311	1962	223	D.4–17	10/92	364	1961
194	B.3–8	12/90	313	1933	224	D.4–18	,,	365	1958
195	B.3–9	,,	316	*	225	D.4–19	11/92	367	1962
196	B.3–10	3/91	318	1937	226	D.4–20	,,	369	*
197	K.3–1	6/91	324	1953	227	R.6–1	11/94	437	1933
198	K.3–2	,,	325	*	228	R.6–2	12/94	438	1943
199	K.3–3	,,	326	1962	229	R.6–3	,,	439	1961
200	K.3–4	7/91	327	1962	230	R.6–4	,,	440	1956
201	K.3–5	,,	328	*	231	R.6–5	,,	441	1939†
202	K.3–6	8/91	329	*	232	R.6–6	1/95	443	1959
203	K.3–7	,,	330	1955	233	R.6–7	,,	444	1958
204	K.3–8	9/91	331	1953	234	R.6–8	2/95	445	1937
205	K.3–9	,,	332	*	235	R.6–9	3/95	447	1933
206	K.3–10	,,	333	*	236	R.6–10	,,	448	1960

* In IW, see Table p. 61.
† Wdn. 5/39, reinstated 1940 to meet wartime engine shortage. Finally wdn 1953.

For many years these engines were at Clapham Junction shunting in the carriage sidings. No 232 had a particularly long spell on this duty from 1915 till 1920, when it went to Eastleigh shops and emerged with a Drummond chimney, being sent elsewhere on the system. Unlike most other lines at this period, LSWR practice was to replace an engine going into works by another of the same class just out of shops. If one happened to go back to its former shed it was purely by chance. Thus over a period of years most engines were seen all over the system on lines which they normally worked

Between 1923, the formative year of the Southern, and 1949, just after the setting up of BR, 23 O2 engines were transferred to the Isle of Wight, and renumbered 14 to 36 inclusive. For this purpose, the steam brake and vacuum ejector, which is the standard braking equipment of this class, had to be replaced by the Westinghouse automatic brake, which has always been the standard system on the Island Section. The donkey pump was mounted on the left-hand side of the smokebox, and the air reservoir on top of the left-hand (i.e., the near side) tank.

Almost immediately after the Grouping, two O2 Class tanks were sent to the Isle of Wight to replace aged Beyer, Peacock 2–4–0Ts. No 206 is seen here at Shanklin in June, 1923, still in LSWR livery. The Westinghouse pump and air reservoir, which were fitted, are prominent

More transfers took place over the years, the last as late as 1949, by which time there were 23 of them. The survivors lasted until the end of steam working in the island in December 1966. They were renumbered into a separate series, W14 to W36, and all subsequently named after Isle of Wight places. No W17 Seaview was formerly 208, and is seen here in Ryde shed just after transfer in 1930

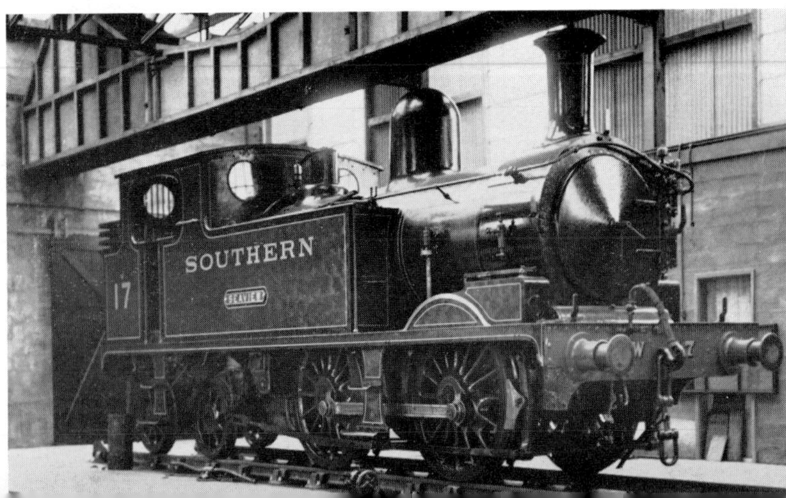

Cast brass nameplates were added to the Island O2s, commencing with No 28 *Ashey* in 1929, and correspondingly the numerals were relegated to the bunker sides. The prefix 'W' entered against the Island engines in this list was borne on each engine repainted prior to 1931, when the general re-numbering scheme abolished all the Section letters. The 'W' was incorporated also in the single cast-brass numberplate which was affixed to the back of the bunker.

LSWR No	*IW No*	*Date transferred from mainland*	*Name*	*Wdn*	*LSWR No*	*IW No*	*Date transferred from mainland*	*Name*	*Wdn*
178	14	1936	*Fishbourne*	1966	206	19	1923	*Osborne*	1955
180	31	1927	*Chale*	1967	208	17	1930	*Seaview*	1966
181	35	1949	*Freshwater*	1966	209	24	1925	*Calbourne*	1967*
184	27	1926	*Merstone*	1966	210	26	,,	*Whitwell*	1966
186	28	,,	*Ashey*	1966	211	20	1923	*Shanklin*	1966
188	23	1925	*Totland*	1955	215	22	1924	*Brading*	1966
190	25	,,	*Godshill*	1962	217	16	1936	*Ventnor*	1966
195	15	1936	*Cowes*	1956	218	33	,,	*Bembridge*	1966
198	36	1949	*Carisbrooke*	1964	219	30	1926	*Shorwell*	1965
201	34	1947	*Newport*	1955	220	18	1930	*Ningwood*	1965
202	29	1926	*Alverstone*	1966	226	32	1928	*Bonchurch*	1964
205	21	1924	*Sandown*	1966					

* No 24 *Calbourne* has been preserved in the Island.

The first two O2s transferred, LSWR Nos 206 and 211, were landed at Ryde Pier Head, and worked for a time in South Western livery. The next two, LSWR Nos 205 and 215 were shipped to St. Helens wharf in sections, and re-assembled by fitters sent from Eastleigh, Subsequent engines were sent to Medina wharf complete, and landed by floating crane.

Nos W27 to W32 were fitted with new Drummond boilers in readiness for their transfer, but between 1936 (first engine concerned No W31) and 8/1938 (last engine concerned No W32) the Drummond boilers were replaced by those of Adams' type. The four transferred in 1936 also had the Adams type boiler.

The bunker capacity of the O2s was on the small side for Island requirements, and proved inconvenient at the height of the season because it required frequent re-coaling. In 8/1932, No W19 *Osborne* was fitted with an extended bunker top, and this was forthwith improved to form a complete extension upwards from the buffer beam, without any increase in frame length.

The first engine thus was No 26 *Whitwell*, booked out of Ryde shops the first week of September, 1932, and later all the O2s including subsequent transfers, were similarly altered. The new bunker held twice as much coal as before (3 tons against $1\frac{1}{2}$), and the total engine weight was increased by $1\frac{1}{2}$ tons to 48 tons 8cwt.

The O2s were not classed for power on their parent section, but from the mid-1930s, those in the Isle of Wight were graded and lettered 'B'. The Island engines were always excellently maintained at a degree of efficiency hardly surpassed in Adams' time.

Many O2s were fitted for pull-and-push working from 1915 onwards, of the original cable and pulley type, and later with the Westinghouse air control system. The last to be so adapted were Nos W35 and W36 on their transfer to the Isle of Wight in 1949. The Westinghouse air compressor (donkey pump) for this purpose was mounted on the left hand side of the smokebox, in the position it occupied on the Isle of Wight engines. From May 1902 to August 1902, No 180 was fitted with Holden's liquid fuel apparatus.

A number of the class was fitted with Drummond boilers, but several reverted to the Adams type, sometimes the boiler being transferred to another engine. In a few instances the conversions and reconversions took place more than once, especially among the Isle of Wight engines. The dates of first fitting of Drummond boilers were: 179 (1939), 181 (1946), 183 (1945), 185 (1931), 191 (1909), 192 (1946), 193 (1958), 194 (1925), 199 (1934), 203 (1927), 204 (1926), 207 (1946), 213 (1929), 214 (1926), 221 (1948), 223 (1907), 224 (1953), 229 (1951), 233 (1926), 236 (1942). W18, W22, W25, W27 to W33 (on transfer to the Isle of Wight or subsequently).

All of the class ultimately received Drummond chimneys, the last to retain the Adams stovepipe being Nos 222 (until 1924), 227 (1923), 228 (1928), 230 (1927), 231 (1924), 232 (1920), 233 (1927), 234 (1928), 235 (1927) and 236 (1918).

Many later transfers had Drummond boilers, as No W27 Merstone *(late 184), but they were found to steam less satisfactorily and most later reverted to the Adams type*

The Isle of Wight engines were eventually provided with enlarged bunkers to give increased coal capacity. No W35 Freshwater *leaves Newport on a Freshwater train in 1953*

Adams' first 4–4–0 design, the 'Steamrollers'. No 382 in original condition

380 Class Mixed Traffic 4–4–0

Total in class: 12. Built: Beyer, Peacock 1879

Following the 46 Class tank engines already described, came a series of 12 tender engines of practically the same dimensions for longer runs. Dubbed 'Steamrollers' by reason of their disc bogie wheels and 'stove pipe' chimneys—a nickname they kept to the end, whereas the tank version appears to have lost this nickname at an early date—these engines were LSWR Nos 380 to 391, built 1879 at Beyer's Gorton Foundry, Manchester, Works Nos respectively 1854 to 1865.

The 380 Class was in many respects a departure from traditional South Western practice, though, as will be noticed from the various illustrations, Adams shared the Beattie liking for outside cylinders. Their principal features were steam brakes (the first ever used on the LSWR), single slide bars, and weight. At the time, they were the heaviest engines on the system, and this is said to have somewhat restricted their activities.

They were at first all stationed at Nine Elms, and did a fair amount of excursion work. Later they were often in evidence on heavy business trains to and from Richmond, but most of their career was spent in the goods links, and for many years they worked the transfer goods and coal trains between Brent sidings, Midland Railway (near Cricklewood) and Battersea yard, where the proximity of a wellknown canine hostel earned them the soubriquet of 'Dog's Home Shunters'.

At the close of the Adams period, most of them were stationed at Exmouth Junction, working thence through Devon and into Cornwall, and at least one was invariably to be found at Strawberry Hill (which was a last refuge as well for many old Beattie engines) for the Wimbledon-Leatherhead goods turns.

The principal dimensions of the 'Steamrollers' were as follows: Outside cylinders 18in × 24in. Wheel diameter, bogie 2ft 6in, coupled 5ft 7in. The boiler was 4in larger in barrel diameter than that of the 'Ironclad' tanks, but the barrel length, boiler pitch and working pressure were the same. Heating surface: 234 $1\frac{5}{8}$in tubes, 1,035sq ft, firebox 101sq ft, total hs 1,136sq ft. The firebox was 6ft 0in long outside (4in longer than that of the tank class), and the grate area 16·96sq ft.

The tender was mounted on six wheels, 3ft $9\frac{3}{4}$in diameter, equally spaced on a 10ft 3in wheelbase, held 2,500 gallons of water, and was provided with the customary footboard and handrail to give access to the rear part, where the tool box and water-filling hole were placed. The engine wheel base was 21ft $8\frac{1}{2}$in, total wheelbase (E. & T.) 40ft 1in, length over buffers (E. & T.) 47ft $9\frac{1}{4}$in, weight in working order, engine 46 tons $1\frac{1}{2}$cwt, tender 30 tons 2 cwt, total 76 tons $13\frac{1}{2}$cwt. Power class was K.

The list of the 380 Class is as follows:

No	*New No*	*Wdn*	*No*	*New No*	*Wdn*
380	0380	1925	386	0386 / 0277*	1924
381	0381	,,	387	0387	1914
382	0382 / 0160*	1924	388	0388 / 0162*	1925
383	0383	1914	389	0389	1914
384	0384	1924	390	0390 / 0337*	1925
385	0385 / 0288*	1924	391	0391	1914

* New number on being reinstated for service, 1914. The other renumberings listed above were done 1902, see text.
Wdn—Withdrawn.

The above engines were painted the dark green goods colour ever since its adoption, which would be about the 1885 period. Previous to this, Adams had

No 381 as rebuilt in 1899 with higher-pitched boiler and tall dome

The last survivor of the class was No 388, by then renumbered 0162, here at Exmouth Junction in 1924. It worked until 1925

varied the Beattie chocolate livery to a rather dull brown tint, lined in green and orange, and this appears to have been the style in which the 'Steamrollers' first took the road. The brass numerals were ultimately taken off to suit the duplicate notation and so roughly was the job done that the outlines remained beneath the transfer numerals with which they were replaced.

The relegation of this class to the duplicate list took place in 1902 to suit the new K10 class engines, and the plan of duplicating by drawing a black line through the existing brass numerals was first practised on this occasion, though it is not known precisely which of the 'Steamrollers' were concerned.

As duplicates, they carried on until 1914, when no fewer than nine were condemned, but of these, five were reprieved to ease the wartime engine shortage. As late as the summer of 1922, Nos 0380/1 were seen still at work at Exmouth Junction, from which shed the last surivor in traffic, No 0162, was working in 1924. They were even then well-groomed, and did not flaunt the sad appearance which became so often the lot of old, and not so old, engines.

The 'Steamrollers' were built, as stated above, with steam brake, but in their later years, they had the vacuum brake complete.

Between 1897 and 1899 Nos 380, 381, and 384 were rebuilt with higher pitched boilers of 160lb pressure.

Adams' first express design of 4–4–0 with 6ft 7in driving wheels, followed in 1880, Nos 135–146. This view shows 144 in original condition

135 Class Express 4–4–0

Total in class: 12. Built: Beyer, Peacock December 1880

Mr Adams' first express passenger engines for the LSWR were of the 4–4–0 type, Nos 135–146 (B.P. Works Nos 1948–59). They had outside cylinders 18in × 24in, coupled wheels 6ft 7in, bogie wheels 3ft 4in, total engine wheelbase 7ft 0in + 6ft 5½in + 8ft 6in = 21ft 11½in. The boiler was 4ft 6in diameter and 10ft 0¾in long pitched with its centre 7ft 4in from rail level, pressed at 140lb per sq in, and contained 234 tubes 1¾in outside diameter, giving 1112sq ft of heating surface, to which the firebox added 111sq ft, total heating surface 1223sq ft. The firebox was 6ft 0in long, and the grate area 17·77sq ft. In working order,

No 136 as re-boilered by Drummond in 1896 with conical smokebox door

the engine weighed 46 tons 8cwt, which was unusually heavy for its time. The tender, mounted on 6 wheels, 3ft $9\frac{3}{4}$in diameter, 10ft 3in total wheelbase, equally divided, held 2,500 gallons of water and $3\frac{1}{2}$ tons of coal, and weighed 30 tons 2cwt. Total weight, engine and tender, 76 tons 10cwt, total length over buffers, 48ft $10\frac{1}{4}$in. The tender was in Beattie's tradition with a footboard and handrail along each side.

In 1896, No 136 was re-boilered with an Adams boiler, and at the same time fitted with a Drummond pattern conical smokebox door, similar to some fitted on his 687 Class goods and M7 class tank engines, and discussed under the latter heading. It is worth noting that after this re-boilering, the height over chimney was 13ft $2\frac{3}{4}$in, a dimension which applied to the great majority of Drummond engines.

Braking equipment comprised steam brake on engine and tender with vacuum ejector for the train.

In 1902, all the engines were transferred to the duplicate list, and in 1914 Nos 135, 139, 140, 143 and 144 were allotted new duplicate numbers.

No	*New No and Date*	*Wdn*	*No*	*New No and Date*	*Wdn*	*No*	*New No and Date*	*Wdn*
135	0135 7/02 0370 4/14	1922	139	0139 9/02 0307 3/14	1925	143	0143 10/02 0312 5/14	1923
136	0136 7/02	1921	140	0140 9/02 0310 5/14	1924	144	0144 10/02 0347 5/14	1922
137	0137 7/02	1921						
138	0138 7/02	1921	141	0141 9/02	1921	145	0145 11/02	1921
			142	0142 10/02	1921	146	0146 11/02	1921

Wdn—Withdrawn.

When new, the '135' Class were on express passenger services from Nine Elms, which they maintained for ten years, before being replaced by later designs.

Five of these engines still survived in 1914, when they were renumbered, No 0143 becoming 0312. It is seen here in Eastleigh yard in 1922, where it had lain since at least 1919, although it was not officially withdrawn from stock until 1923

No 449 as originally built—Adams 445 Class

445 Class Express 4–4–0

Total in Class: 12. Built: R. Stephenson 1883

In 1883, Adams produced a 4-coupled express type which was in some respects an enlargement of the 135 Class, having 6in larger coupled wheels. Together the engine and tender were 3ft 1¼in longer and 8 tons 7cwt heavier, but the engine itself was actually 6cwt lighter than No 135 and the tube heating surface was less, though that of the firebox was somewhat increased. The new class comprised Nos 445–56 (R.S. Works Nos. 2535–46) and the chief dimensions were as follows:

Bogie wheels 3ft 7in, coupled 7ft 1in; outside cylinders 18in × 24in. Working pressure 160lb per sq in. Boiler 4ft 4in × 10ft 2½in. Length of outside firebox 6ft 0in, centre-line of boiler 7ft 9in above rail. Heating surface 1,161sq ft, of which 216 tubes 1¾in diameter provided 1,043sq ft and the firebox 118sq ft. The grate area was 17sq ft. The tender ran on six wheels 3ft 9¾in diameter and held 2,800 gallons. Total wheelbase of engine and tender 43ft 5⅝in; front overhang 4ft 0¾in, rear overhang 4ft 5in, overall length 51ft 11⅜in. Weight in wo (E) 46 tons 2cwt (T) 32 tons 5cwt, total 78 tons 7cwt. Power class K.

In May, 1884, a Webb 3-cylinder compound of his 6ft 6in 'Experiment' class (LNWR) was borrowed by Adams for trials against engines of the 445 Class. The LNWR engine, No 300 *Compound*, worked two complete round trips, Waterloo-Exeter-Waterloo against LSW locomotives Nos 449 and 454. The LNW compound did not put up a record for economy in fuel.

In February, 1888, No 446 was converted (under order N1) to a 2-cylinder compound on the Worsdell-von-Borries system, for which purpose the left-hand cylinder was retained and a right-hand low pressure cylinder of 26in diameter

No 448 after receiving a new boiler with tall dome, and unusual LSWR insignia on the splasher (left); when photographed at Guildford in 1922, again had the original type of small dome

was fitted, and the motion was modified to give a longer valve travel. After running thus for three years, new simple cylinders of the original diameter were refitted in February, 1891. The results did not justify the building of new engines of the N1 Class.

For the first nine years, the 445 Class worked on the London-Southampton services and even in later years were rarely to be seen west of Salisbury.

No	*Rebuilt*†	*New No and Date*	*Wdn*	*No*	*Rebuilt*†	*New No and Date*	*Wdn*
445	—	0445 (1911)	1926	450	—	0450 (1911)	1925
446	1888* 1891*	0446 (1911)	1925	451	1896	0451 (1911)	1925
				452	—	0452 (1911)	1926
447	1896	0447 (1911)	1926	453	—	0453 (1908)	1925
448	1894	0448 (1910) 448A (1924)	1925	454	—	0454 (1908)	1925
				455	1895	0455 (1908)	1925
449	1893	0449 (1910)	1925	456	—	0456 (1908)	1925

* Experimental compound between these dates.
† Except where starred*, this infers new boilers substantially of the original design.
Wdn=Withdrawn.

ENGINE SUMMARY

No 0451 was seen in 1925 at Eastleigh Works Yard next to its successor (Drummond 4–6–0 **No 451**) both awaiting breaking up. **No 0452** actually lasted several months longer than the Drummond 4–6–0 which succeeded to its original number.

Nos 446 and **451** were fitted with Drummond boilers, in 1907 and 1909 respectively which they carried until withdrawal. Several of the engines received new boilers of Adams design but with taller dome casings, greatly improving their appearance.

All except **Nos 0447** and **0455** eventually had Drummond chimneys, but these two retained the Adams stovepipes to the end. **Nos 0445, 0447,** and **0451** were the only ones to receive Southern livery.

It will be noted that all these 445 Class engines put in over 40 years' work, like many other Adams classes, showing that Adams was well in front of the requirements of his day.

Only three of the class, Nos 0445, 0447 and 0451, survived to be repainted in SR colours, and 0447 even managed to retain its stovepipe chimney, as seen from its cab

No 0451 at Eastleigh in 1921, rebuilt with Drummond boiler, which not only spoiled its appearance, but also its efficiency. These boilers, although suited to Drummond's own engines, never seemed to steam so well when applied to Adams' types

No 526, the Exhibition engine of 460 class

460 Class Express 4–4–0

Total in class: 21. Built: Neilson, and Robert Stephenson 1884 and 1887

1884	(June onwards) **Nos 147, 470-8,** R. Stephenson & Co. (2561-70) ...	10
	(September onwards) **Nos 460-9,** Neilson & Co. (3190–9)	10
1887	**No 526,** R. Stephenson & Co. (2650)	1
	Total	21

In 1884, Adams put in service some more express engines, Nos 147 and 460–78, which closely resembled his 135 Class of 1880. They were somewhat lighter, though the weight on the coupled wheels was greater and a larger tender was provided. In 1886–7, Stephenson built, at their own expense, one more engine of the Class here reviewed for the exhibition at Newcastle in Queen Victoria's Jubilee Year (1887), and gained a gold medal. This engine was purchased by the LSWR and numbered 526, and the award was advertised on elliptical plates on the cab sides until the last few years of her existence.

The leading dimensions of the 460 Class (power class: K) were:

Cylinders 18in × 24in, bogie wheels 3ft 4in diameter, coupled wheels 6ft 7in. Boiler 4ft 4in × 10ft 2½in, pressed at 160lb per sq in, and pitched 7ft 4in above rail; outside firebox 6ft 0in long. The boiler contained 218 tubes, 1¾in outside diameter, giving a heating surface of 1,051sq ft, to which the firebox added 111·75sq ft, total heating surface 1,162·75sq ft. Grate area 17·6sq ft. Weight in working order (E) 45 tons 15 cwt, (T) 28 tons 18cwt; total 74 tons 13cwt. The water capacity of the tender was originally 2,350 gallons, but later many had 2,800 gallon tenders substituted.

No	*New No and Date*	*Wdn*	*No*	*New No and Date*	*Wdn*	*No*	*New No and Date*	*Wdn*
147	0147 (1908)	1927	466	0466 (1912)	1928	473	0473 (1923)	1929
460	0460 (1912)	1929	467	0467 (1912)	1929	474	0474 (1923)	1929
461	0461 (1912)	1926	468	0468 (1912)	1928	475	0475 (1924)	1926
462	0462 (1912)	1926	469	0469 (1912)	1927	476	0476 (1924)	1926
463	0463 (1912)	1927	470	0470 (1912)	1929	477	0477 (1924)	1927
464	0464 (1912)	1928	471	0471 (1912)	1928	478	0478 (1924)	1929
465	0465 (1912)	1925	472	0472 (1912)	1928	526	——	1928

No 477 at Andover in 1922

With this class Adams appears to have changed dome design, now much taller and stately. There evolved two distinct varieties, a taller one as carried by 0469, the more common, but the shapely edifice on No 0147, at Eastleigh in 1923 is possibly even finer

ENGINE SUMMARY

Nos 0473 and **526** were fitted 1926 with Drummond boilers respectively off **Nos 0446** and **0451** of 445 Class.

No 526 was handed over to the LSWR in November, 1887, after the close of the Newcastle Exhibition, and a few months later, on 5th March, 1888, she worked the official train opening the new direct service to Bournemouth.

Unlike the 445 Class, all of the 460s had received Drummond chimneys at least by 1916.

All but Nos. 0461, 0465, and 0475, received Southern livery.

These engines at the close of the Adams period were commonly seen on the Salisbury-Exeter lighter trains, whereas the 7-footers rarely penetrated West of Salisbury.

Several remained on main line duties in North Devon until withdrawn, and Nos 0471, 0472 and 526 finished up at Wadebridge depot. The late Colonel Stephens wished to obtain some of these engines for his various light railways, but unfortunately the negotiations never materialised.

Adams 0–6–0 No 434 as built

395 Class Goods 0–6–0

Total in class: 70. Built: Neilson, 1881-1886.

1881	(delivery commenced November), 395–9 (2747–51)	5
1882	400–6 (2752–8)	7
1883	(March, April) 153–9, 163–7 (2939–50)	24
	(April, May, June), 433–44 (2956–67)	
1885	(delivery commenced October), 496–515 (3376–95)	34
	27–30, 69, 71, 101/5/34/48 (3453–62)	
1886	(delivery completed February), 168/72/4/5 (3463–6)	
	Total	70

Adams' first main line goods engine appeared at the close of 1881. The inside cylinders were 17½in × 26in, and the wheels 5ft 1in diameter. The boiler barrel 4ft 4in × 10ft 6in, pitched with its centre-line 7ft 0in above rail level, contained 218 tubes, 1¾in outside diameter, giving 1,079sq ft of heating surface, to which the firebox added 108sq ft, total heating surface, 1,187sq ft. The firebox was 5ft 10in long outside, and the grate area was 17·8sq ft. The tender ran on 6 wheels, 3ft 9¾in diameter, held 2,500 gallons of water, and perpetuated Beattie's characteristic handrail and footboard, which extended nearly the entire length of the tender and so gave access to the tank filling holes at the extreme far corners.

No 0397 at Strawberry Hill in 1922

No 3506 at Eastleigh in 1936 fitted with a Kirtley boiler, taken from a former London, Chatham & Dover 4–4–0

The engines built in 1885/6 were heavier, principally owing to an increase in length at the front end, but the tenders were identical throughout the various lots, and weighed 28 tons 13cwt in working order. The dimensional differences between locomotives of the 395 Class, 1881–3, and those of the 496 Class, 1885–6, as the two variants were sometimes called, are tabulated hereunder. Constructional differences included single slide-bars instead of the four bar arrangement of the 1881–3 engines. Power class was G.

	395 *Class*		**496** *Class*	
Front overhang	6ft 6½in		7ft 10in	
Overall length	48ft 0¾in		49ft 4¼in	
Weight on leading wheels	12 tons	16cwt	13 tons	17cwt
,, ,, driving ,,	13	12	13	16
,, ,, trailing ,,	11	4	11	1
Total weight engine only	37	12	38	14
Total weight engine and tender	66	5	67	7

During World War I, 50 of them were commandeered by the Government and sent abroad to the Middle East. None of them ever returned. They were partly replaced on the LSWR by the restoration of some old Beattie engines from Eastleigh scrapyard, as already detailed, and by the borrowing of seven Stirling 0–6–0s from the Great Northern, and three Kirtley 0–6–0s, Nos 2783–2785, from the Midland. The latter spent some of their time at Guildford, the GNR engines being divided mainly between Strawberry Hill and Guildford.

No 0155 with Drummond boiler, at Feltham in 1925

Although they spent three years on the LSWR they retained the old Companies' initials and number.

No	*New No and Date*	*Disposal*
27	027 (1904)	To Palestine 1917, sold 1929.
28	028 (1904)	To Palestine 1917, sold 1929.
29	029 (1904) 3029 (1935)	—
30	030 (1904)	To Palestine 1917, sold 1929.
69	83 (1889) 083 (1908) 3083 (1935)	—
71	84 (1889) 084 (1908)	To Palestine 1916, sold 1929.
101	0101 (1908) 3101 (1933)	—
105	0105 (1905)	Sunk in transit to Palestine, 1918.
134	0134 (1904)	To Serbia 1916.
148	0148 (1904)	To Palestine 1916, sold 1929.
153*	0153 (1902)	Withdrawn 1933.
154	0154 (1903) 3154 (1933)	—
155	0155 (1903) 3155 (1935)	—
156	0156 (1903)	To Mesopotamia 1917.
157	0157 (1903)	To Serbian State Railway, No 21, 1916.
158	0158 (1903)	To Palestine 1917, sold 1929.
159	0159 (1903)	To Palestine 1916, sold 1929.
163	0163 (1903) 3163 (1932)	—
164	0164 (1903)	To Palestine 1916, sold 1929.
165	0165 (1903)	Sunk in transit to Palestine, 1918.
166	0166 (1904)	To Palestine 1916; out of service 1937; written off 1944.
167	0167 (1904) 3167 (1931)	—
168	0168 (1904)	To Palestine 1918, sold 1929.
172	0172 (1904)	To Palestine 1916, sold 1929.
174	0174 (1906)	To Mesopotamia 1917.
175	0175 (1906)	To Serbian State Railway, No 22, 1916.

* First of class cut up at Eastleigh.

No	*New No and Date*	*Disposal*
395	0395 (1903)	To Palestine 1916, written off 1944.
396	0396 (1903)	To Palestine 1917, sold 1929.
397	0397 (1903) 3397 (1931)	—
398	0398 (1903)	To Palestine 1917, withdrawn 1937, written off 1944.
399	0399 (1903)	To Palestine 1916, sold 1929.
400	0400 (1903) 3400 (1935)	—
401	0401 (1903)	To Palestine 1916, sold 1929.
402	0402 (1903)	To Mesopotamia 1917.
403	0403 (1906)	To Mesopotamia 1917.
404	0404 (1906)	Sunk in transit to Palestine 1918.
405	0405 (1906)	To Palestine 1916; withdrawn 1937; written off 1944.
406	0406 (1906)	Sunk in transit to Palestine 1918.
433	0433 (1905) 3433 (1935)	—
434	0434 (1905)	To Palestine, thence to Mesopotamia 1918.
435	0435 (1906)	To Serbian State Railway, No 23, 1916.
436	0436 (1906) 436A (1924) 0436 (1924) 3436 (1932)	—
437	0437 (1906)	To Palestine, thence to Mesopotamia 1918.
438	0438 (1907)	To Palestine 1917, sold 1929.
439	0439 (1907) 3439 (1932)	—
440	0440 (1907) 3440 (1935)	—
441	0441 (1907) 3441 (1935)	—
442	0442 (1907) 3442 (1931)	—
443	0443 (1911)	To Mesopotamia 1917.
444	0444 (1911)	To Palestine 1917, withdrawn 1937; written off 1944.

No 436A in the short-lived style of renumbering duplicate engines immediately after the Grouping. This was quickly followed by a reversion to the LSWR system, ie 0436, eventually superseded by the addition of 3000

No 508 at Palestine Railway works, Qishon, awaiting cutting up in 1944

No	*New No and Date*	*Disposal*
496	0496 (1921) 496A (1924) 0496 (1924) 3496 (1933)	—
497	—	To Palestine 1917, sold 1929.
498	—	To Mesopotamia 1917.
499	—	To Palestine 1917, sold 1929.
500	—	To Mesopotamia 1917.
501	—	To Palestine 1917; not erected; sold 1929.
502	—	To Palestine 1916, sold 1929.
503	—	To Palestine 1917, withdrawn 1937; written off 1944.

No	*New No and Date*	*Disposal*	*No*	*New No and Date*	*Disposal*
504	—	To Mesopotamia 1917.	510	—	To Palestine 1916, sold 1929.
505	—	To Mesopotamia 1917.	511	—	To Serbian State Railway, No 24.
506	0506 (1920) 3506 (1931)	—	512	—	To Palestine, thence to Mesopotamia 1918.
507	—	To Palestine 1916, sold 1929.	513	—	To Palestine 1916, sold 1929.
508	—	To Palestine 1917, withdrawn 1937; written off 1944.	514	—	To Palestine 1917, sold 1919.
509	0509 (1920) 3509 (1935)	—	515	0515 (1921)	Cut up at Eastleigh, 11/33.

The later history of the twenty engines which remained in this country is shown in a separate table.

Nos 164, 436 and **515** were re-boilered by Drummond with boilers having lock-up safety-valves on the dome: but **No 436** gave up its boiler later to **No 155**, and **No 515** had also had an Adams boiler re-fitted in later 1919 or early 1920. **No 164** was working in Palestine with its Drummond boiler. There were later several interchange of boilers with other engines of the class. Longhedge boilers off London, Chatham & Dover Railway 4–4–0 engines previously scrapped were fitted 11/29 to **Nos 083** and **0515,** and to **No 0433** 9/28. The boiler from **No 0515** (scrapped 1933) was transferred 9/34 to **No 3506. Nos 3154, 3440** and **3506** have 3300-gallon tenders off scrapped A12 Class 0–4–2 engines. **No 3154** left Eastleigh works 8/48 as BR **No 30567** with a LCDR boiler, and an Adams 3300-gallons tender.

No 3509 was temporarily fitted, 6/37, with I3 Class (ex-LBSC) short chimney for Will Hay's film 'Oh! Mr Porter!'

When new, the engines had smokeboxes with sloping fronts, but many have had new smokeboxes with vertical fronts.

The 18 survivors taken over by BR were given entirely new numbers, 30564–30581. No 30574, late 3436, here at Guildford in 1954, lasted until 1957

The engines lost in transit to Palestine were in the ss *Arabic*, torpedoed in the Mediterranean. Those that worked in Palestine had an 'A' after their numbers to prevent confusion with Egyptian engines with the same numbers. The cab roof on these was extended, and Nos 28A and 168A were provided with extended smokeboxes at Bulac Works in 1919. The last of these was scrapped at the Qishon Works of the Palestine Railways in January, 1945, having been withdrawn many years previously. The only traces then remaining were a number of tenders, some of which had been used by the Egyptian State Railways as water carriers in the Western Desert. The engines were actually taken over by the War Dept. in Egypt.

Subsequent history of the surviving engines is as tabulated:

SR number	*Renumbered by BR*	*Wdn*	*SR number*	*Renumbered by BR*	*Wdn*
3029	30564	1958	3433	30573	1956
3083	30565	1953	3436	30574	1957
3101	30566	1959	3439	30575	1958
0153*	—	1933	3440	30576	1950
3154	30567	1959	3441	30577	1956
3155	30568	1958	3442	30578	1957
3163	30569	1956	3496	30579	1956
3167	30570	1956	3506	30580	1957
3397	30571	1953	3509	30581	1953
3400	30572	1957	0515*	—	1933

* Never renumbered in 30xxx series

It will be noted that this was an exceptionally long lived class, so far as the engines which were retained by the LSWR were concerned. Neilson & Co. carried a well deserved reputation for the longevity of their products.

A12 & O4 Classes Mixed Traffic 0–4–2

Total in classes: 90. Built: L.S.W.R., Neilson, Glasgow 1887–1895

Until 1887, Adams had obtained all new engines from outside contractors, but in that year locomotive construction was recommenced in the Company's Works at Nine Elms. The first engines put in hand were those of the 527 or A12 Class, more generally referred to as the 'Jubilees', from the fact that they were introduced in 1887, the fiftieth year of Queen Victoria's reign.

These engines were a striking departure from anything previously built for the LSWR, and for that matter on few other British railways. The brothers Stirling had built some similar engines for the Glasgow & South Western and the Great Northern, and Stroudley of the LBSCR, culminating in the famous 'Gladstones', but these were in a somewhat different category, being essentially express engines, whereas Adams new design for the LSWR was intended for mixed traffic duties. The engines were principally engaged on heavy excursion and troop special services, in addition to passenger trains in the Central and North Devon districts, besides working fast goods services to the West of England, Southampton and Weymouth.

In later years they were much used on local freight and miscellaneous work, but until well after the Grouping a fleet of them was maintained at Guildford for the busy fast residential services to Waterloo.

These engines, of power Class J, had inside cylinders, 18in × 26in with the steam chests underneath, as in Stroudley's 'Gladstones'. The coupled wheels were 6ft 0in and the trailing wheels 4ft 0in diameter. The latter had outside axleboxes, with springs situated behind the frames in all the engines except the first, No 527, the trailing springs of which were placed outside.

The boiler barrel was 4ft 4in diameter × 11ft 0in, pitched 7ft 6in above the rails, pressed at 160lb per sq in and tubed with 216 tubes, 1$\frac{3}{4}$in outside diameter, giving 1,121sq ft of heating surface, to which the firebox added 110sq ft, total heating surface 1,231sq ft. Grate area 17sq ft. Firebox 6ft 0in long outside. Weight of engine in working order 43 tons 8cwt.

These engines were built in two main batches, of which the first, comprising Nos. 527–56, was a Nine Elms production. The thirty engines concerned had screw reversing gear, and all, except the last three, Nos 554–6, had to make do with tenders from old Beyer, Peacock goods engines introduced by Adams' immediate predecessors.

At a very much later date, the tenders in question were replaced by Adams tenders which had become redundant through the scrapping of their own proper engines, e.g. 527 then took the tender from No 0147 (460 Class), 532 from No 0463 and so on.

Nos 554–6 were favoured with new tenders from the start, capacity 3,300 gallons, weight (full) 32 tons, which brought the combined weight of engine and tender to 75 tons 8cwt.

No 555 is shown here in early days, fitted with Westinghouse brake equipment. It had the distinction of working Queen Victoria's funeral train from Gosport to Fareham.

No 529 at Eastleigh in 1924. This was one of the first engines to be repainted in SR colours, and was done so before the decision to prefix LSWR engines with the letter 'E' had been decided upon

The above 30 engines having proved very satisfactory, Adams put on order another 60, officially Classed O4 and allotted to the numerical range 597 to 656, of which Nos 607 to 646 were built by Neilson, Glasgow, and the remainder at Nine Elms.

This new lot differed from the original class in certain details, notably the steam chest, which was now placed between, instead of below, the cylinders. Also, the motion was now reversible by lever, and the engine weighed just over a ton less than its prototype. A minor distinction was that, henceforth, brass beading adorned the rims of the splashers, but this embellishment succumbed to Drummond austerity from 1900 onwards, though a few engines such as 637 and 643 retained it to the end of their existence.

The first 20 engines, Nos 527–46 were fitted with vacuum brake complete, the other 70 had steam brake and vacuum ejector. Nos 529, 534, 538, 543, 555, 556, had Westinghouse donkey pump and control in addition, and 538, 555 are listed with this equipment in the official stock list dated as recently as 1st January, 1931.

In the accompanying table, the seven engines starred* are correctly shown as withdrawn January, 1939, though one lasted till December, 1948. The explanation is, of course, that owing to the demand for engine power due to the outbreak of war, the locomotives affected were reprieved and restored to traffic in the same manner as other locomotives had been reinstated during the first World War.

In addition to breaking new ground in the realm of design, Adams' 'Jubilees' introduced the LSWR to a style of brass number-plate which he had already adopted on the Great Eastern Railway. Commencing with No 527, the individual brass numerals which had distinguished his earlier LSWR engines were superseded by the new and handsome cast plate that displayed, in addition to the number, the historically valuable particulars of date and works of origin. For the next ten years, this type of plate was used for all new construction, as well as for some of Beattie's engines which Adams rebuilt, and even, in the form of a fresh casting, for the same rebuilds when relegated to the duplicate list. It seems a pity that Drummond had to discard such splendid items of brassware, the red background and high polish of which so greatly set off the ever well-groomed appearance of Adams engines.

No	Order No	Date	Works No	Wdn	No	Works No	Date	Wdn	No	Works or Order No	Date	Works No	Wdn
527	A.12–1	5/87	244	1930	607	4506†	1892	1932	637	4536†	1893	—	1946
528	A.12–2	10/87	245	1929	608	4507	,,	1932	638	4537	,,	—	1947
529	A.12–3	,,	246	1928	609	4508	,,	1947	639	4538	,,	—	1933
530	A.12–4	11/87	247	1931	610	4509	,,	1932	640	4539	,,	—	1937
531	A.12–5	,,	248	1929	611	4510	,,	1937	641	4540	,,	—	1945
532	A.12–6	12/87	249	1929	612	4511	,,	1946	642*	4541	,,	—	1947
533	A.12–7	,,	250	1929	613*	4512	,,	1946	643	4542	,,	—	1947
534	A.12–8	,,	251	1931	614	4513	,,	1947	644*	4543	,,	—	1946
535	A.12–9	,,	252	1928	615	4514	,,	1946	645	4544	,,	—	1933
536	A.12–10	,,	253	1929	616	4515	,,	1936	646	4545	,,	—	1939
537	E.1–1	3/88	254	1929	617	4516	,,	1936	597	O.4–1	12/93	400	1947
538	E.1–2	,,	255	1931	618	4517	,,	1948	598	O.4–2	,,	401	1947
539	E.1–3	4/88	256	1930	619	4518	,,	1936	599	O.4–3	,,	404	1946
540	E.1–4	,,	257	1929	620*	4519	,,	1946	600	O.4–4	,,	405	1946
541	E.1–5	5/88	258	1931	621	4520	,,	1935	601	O.4–5	2/94	408	1934
542	E.1–6	6/88	260	1928	622	4521	1893	1936	602	O.4–6	3/94	409	1933
543	E.1–7	,,	261	1929	623	4522	1892	1946	603	O.4–7	,,	410	1935
544	E.1–8	,,	262	1929	624*	4523	1893	1947	604	O.4–8	,,	411	1933
545	E.1–9	,,	263	1931	625*	4524	,,	1947	605	O.4–9	,,	412	1936
546	E.1–10	,,	264	1930	626	4525	,,	1933	606	O.4–10	4/94	414	1946
547	M.2–1	6/89	276	1929	627	4526	,,	1948	647	K.6–1	11/94	434	1933
548	M.2–2	,,	277	1928	628	4527	,,	1938	648	K.6–2	,,	435	1947
549	M.2–3	,,	278	1929	629*	4528	,,	1948	649	K.6–3	,,	436	1946
550	M.2–4	10/89	281	1929	630	4529	,,	1947	650	K.6–4	1/95	442	1938
551	M.2–5	,,	282	1932	631	4530	,,	1933	651	K.6–5	3/95	446	1933
552	M.2–6	11/89	283	1928	632	4531	,,	1937	652	K.6–6	,,	449	1947
553	M.2–7	12/89	285	1928	633	4532	,,	1933	653	K.6–7	4/95	450	1932
554	M.2–8	,,	286	1931	634	4533	,,	1947	654	K.6–8	,,	451	1947
555	M.2–9	,,	287	1944	635	4534	,,	1935	655	K.6–9	,,	452	1936
556	M.2–10	,,	288	1929	636	4535	,,	1948	656	K.6–10	5/95	453	1932

Wdn—Withdrawn.
* Engine wdn 1/39, reinstated 10/39.
† This number and those below are Neilson's Works Nos.
‡ Represents the sequence of construction at Nine Elms from engine No 527, the 244th engine built there.

No 622 at Salisbury in 1924, understood to have been the only engine of the class ever to have worked the famous 11.00 from Waterloo to the West of England in one emergency. Although the class could do almost anything, seldom were they required for main line top link duties.

In common with all of Adams classes, some engines inevitably received Drummond boilers. This view shows No 652 at Windsor in 1930

Nos 542, 544, 622, 636, 644, 645, and **652** were re-boilered with Drummond boilers between 1925 and 1927, some of which were transferred to other engines of the class in later years.

Nos 545, 546 in 1897 had tenders respectively Nos 296A and 230, both of Beattie build.

No 555, with Westinghouse brake control, worked the Westinghouse-fitted LBSCR royal train conveying the body of Queen Victoria from Royal Clarence Yard, Gosport, to Fareham, 2nd February, 1901, and there handed over to LBSC B4 4–4–0 No 54 *Empress* for the journey to Victoria via Cosham, Havant and the Horsham line.

No 555 was renumbered **3555** in the SR duplicate list, 2/42, to make room for one of Mr Bulleid's Q1-Class 0–6–0s, which were intended to occupy Nos 550 onwards, but appeared instead in the 'C' numeration. The particular Q1 concerned thereupon became C6, and the Adams engine, after only 3 days as **No 3555,** was restored to its original number.

Nos 599, 614, 618, 625, 638 were lent to the War Dept. in 1942. **No 625** was returned in 1945, the others in 1943.

No 643 was used in preparation of a cine film, 10/34, and appeared at Holborn Viaduct station lettered 'LSWR' for the purpose.

Nos 625, 638 were used as air-raid shelters at Eastleigh in World War II. For this purpose, they were stood over pits and surrounded by a wall of sandbags.

No 646, after withdrawal from service, was used for 5 years as a portable boiler at Eastleigh.

No 612 was converted to stationary boiler at Eastleigh under **No DS3191** and not cut up until November 1951, then the last of the class in existence.

All eventually acquired Drummond chimneys, the last to retain the Adams stove pipes being Nos 615 (until 1919), 648 (1919), 649 (1920), 652 (1926), 653 (1924), 654 (1925), and 655 (1925).

The brass beading round the splashers was gradually removed from most engines, but a few of them, such as Nos 551, 622, 633, 637, 643, 644 and 646 retained it well into the 1920's.

The first of the large Adams 4–4–0s, Class X2 No 577, in original condition

X2, T3, T6 & X6 Classes Standard Express 4–4–0

Total in classes: 60. Built: LSWR

In June, 1890, there appeared from Nine Elms the first of an entirely new range of 4–4–0 express engines, which ultimately totalled 60 units, divided into four distinct classes, viz., X2, T3, T6 and X6 in chronological order. In order of their categories, X2 and T6 and 7ft 1in wheels, and were officially regarded as one class, and T3 and X6 and 6ft 7in wheels, no doubt with a view to their employment on the heavy grades west of Salisbury for which it had for years been the rule to use a 6in smaller driving wheel.

All four classes lasted to become thoroughly familiar SR engines, and in their time, were called upon for almost every kind of passenger work, beginning with main line express from which even Drummond's extensive classes did not entirely displace them. The details of the Adams standard 4–4–0s, simple, logical and efficient, were typical of the best practice of the 'nineties, and in handsome appearance and splendid finish they equalled any similar type of engine on the British roads.

The classes are here reviewed chronologically and the dimensional table has been arranged to show precisely which dimensions were common as between one type and the other. Features common to all included a three-point suspension of the engines' super-structure, viz. at the centre of the Adams' bogie, and by an equalising beam each side between the fore and the rear pair of coupled wheels.

This suspension system, in conjunction with a long wheelbase, minimised the tendency to unsteadiness inherent in all outside cylinder engines, and ensured very smooth running. In recent years, the equalising beams were removed, and the riding qualities of the engines correspondingly suffered.

Other details common throughout included overhead slide bars, steam brake and vacuum ejector, and the standard Adams tender, mounted on six wheels, 3ft 9¾in diameter, equally spaced on a 13ft wheelbase. This type of tender held 3,300 gallons of water, 5 tons of coal, and weighed 10 tons 12½cwt + 10 tons 12½cwt + 11 tons 19cwt, total 33 tons 4cwt in working order.

All four classes were built at Nine Elms Works, and the later examples were completed under Drummond, who introduced variations detailed later. The power classification was 'I' throughout.

Class X2 of 1890–92, Nos. 577–596 (20)

From this inaugural lot, the entire range developed. With 7ft driving wheels, it was a considerable advance on Adams' 445 Class of 1883, and the first engine underwent careful trials at which Adams was assisted by his Works Manager, W. F. Pettigrew, afterwards Locomotive Superintendent of the Furness Railway, and the author of the celebrated 'Manual of Locomotive Engineering', in which full details of performances may be found.

Pettigrew considered the X2 engines to be amongst the most powerful and economical in the world.

Nos 587–596 of this lot were built to order F3, but all 20 were officially Classed X2. With the exception that Nos 577–581 had a separate splasher casing, whereas the others had small segmental covers to enclose the top centres of the coupling rods, the 20 engines were uniform.

This class differed from the earlier Adams express engines by having sandboxes below the footplate, and the plain quadrant splashers were adorned with a device consisting of the Companys' intertwined initials. In Adams' time, and after, the pistons were fitted with tail rods which projected through a stuffing box in the front cylinder cover, but piston tail rods were not part of Drummond's policy, and as occasion offered, this type of piston head was superseded.

Class T3 of 1892–93, Nos. 557–576 (20)

This design was based on Class X2, and principally differed in having 6ft 7in driving wheels, and a firebox 6in longer. Correlated dimensions, such as boiler pitch, were altered to suit, and they may be studied in the comparative table appended.

T3 engines were intended to relieve the existing Adams 6ft 7in 4–4–0s of the 460 Class, which had already been in traffic some eight years, and in this respect

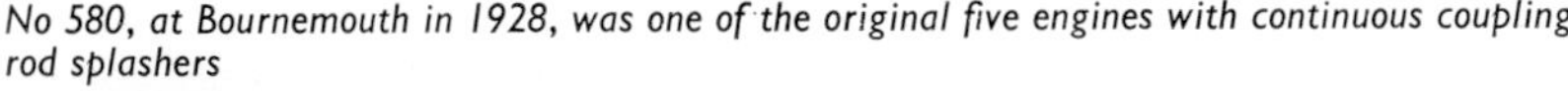

No 580, at Bournemouth in 1928, was one of the original five engines with continuous coupling rod splashers

they were a very considerable advance, as reference back to p. 69 will readily indicate.

As well as being a notable design for their day, the T3s were more generally usable than the X2s, owing to the smaller wheel diameter, and no doubt this widened scope kept the T3s in service longer than the 7-footers on which they were based.

Class T6, of 1895–96, Nos. 677–686 (10)

This was substantially Class X2 with the 6in longer firebox adopted in Class T3, but the boiler tubes of Class T6 were fewer in number, with corresponding reductions in tubular and total heating surface.

Class T6 had certain new features, such as a longer smokebox, a new layout of the running plate, and a smooth one-piece cast-iron chimney, all of which considerably smartened their appearance. Notable omissions, probably due to Drummond, were the piston tailrods, and the small independent splashers which covered the bogie wheels of the earlier classes. Details inspired by Drummond included, probably the coal rails above the tender coping, the Company's coat-of-arms on the driving splashers, and certainly the large and small hooters which were fitted to at least one engine of this Class, No 686, instead of the customary pair of whistles.

Class X6, of 189–596, Nos. 657–666 (10)

This class appeared more or less simultaneously with Class T6, and it was really a duplicate thereof except that the coupled wheels were 6in smaller in diameter, and correlated dimensions such as boiler pitch, and bogie wheel diameter, were adjusted to suit. The X6s appear to have come under Drummond's influence rather more than the T6s, and they consequently displayed the Drummond smooth number plate, and were devoid of brass beading.

This class was the first to bear the contracted initials, 'SWR' on the tender, and the X6 engines were painted in the Drummond style, viz., a light brown edging separated from the green body colour by two white lines. The Adams practice of stamping the construction date on the ends of the axles was maintained for Nos 657–60, but thereafter no date of any kind appeared on further engines turned out from Nine Elms.

It is likely that Adams intended to build 20 of this class, since the numerical range was vacant up to 677, Class T6, but Drummond did not continue the X6s, and the blank numbers were ultimately filled by the M7 0-4-4Ts of his own design.

No 682 of Class T6 passing Wimbledon in 1925

No 558 of Class T3, rebuilt with Drummond boiler, at Eastleigh in 1930

In this instance again, a year or more usually elapsed between withdrawal and scrapping. No 658, which had a Drummond boiler fitted by August, 1922 and retained it to the end, was the last in service of all the numerous Adams 4-4-0 engines.

It is interesting that X2 and T3 engines were not cut up immediately they were withdrawn. Examples are detailed in the Engine Summary, and some of the engines concerned stood for the best part of a year, usually on the 'dead' line at the back of Eastleigh Shed. T3 No 563, one of the engines affected, was restored to 'Adams' condition in 1948 and is now preserved in Clapham Museum.

Class	*X2*	*T3*	*T6*	*X6*
Cylinders (*in*)	19′ × 26″	←	←	←
Wheel diameter:				
Bogie	3′ 9¾″	3′ 7″	3′ 9¾″	3′ 7″
Driving	7′ 1″	6′ 7″	7′ 1″	6′ 7″
Boiler:				
Barrel Diameter	4′ 4″	←	←	←
,, Length	11′ 0″	←	←	←
Wkg. Press. (*lb psi*) ...	175	←	←	←
Pitch above rail	7′ 9″	7′ 6″	7′ 9″	7′ 6″
Firebox, length outside ...	6′ 4″	6′ 10″	←	←
Tubes, how many	230	←	220	230
,, Diameter	1¾″	←	←	←
Heating Surface (*sq ft*)				
Tubes	1,193·7	1,193·7	1,141·7	1,193·7
Firebox	114·8	122·1	122·1	122·1
Total	1,308·5	1,315·8	1,263·8	1,315·8
Grate area (*sq ft*)	18	19·75	19·65	←
Wheelbase:				
Bogie	7′ 6″	←	←	←
Coupled	8′ 6″	9′ 0″	←	←
Total (*Engine*)	23′ 0″	23′ 6″	23′ 9″	←
,, (*E. and T.*)	44′ 3⅛″	44′ 9⅛″	45′ 0⅛″	←
Over Buffers	53′ 8⅜″	54′ 2⅜″	54′ 5⅜″	←
Weight *wo*:				
Engine	48t 13½c	48t 11c	50t 2½c	49t 13c
E. and T.	81t 17½c	81t 15c	83t 6½c	82t 17c

The arrow ← repeats the dimension to which it points.
Boiler barrel dimensions are minimum external diameter × length from tube-plate to throat plate.

No	Order No	Date	Nine Elms Works No	Wdn	No	Order No	Date	Nine Elms Works No	Wdn
577	X.2–1	6/90	300	1933	557	T.3–1	12/92	371	1936
578	X.2–2	12/90	312	,,	558	T.3–2	,,	373	1931
579	X.2–3	,,	314	1932	559	T.3–3	,,	375	,,
580	X.2–4	,,	315	1933	560	T.3–4	2/93	377	1932
581	X.2–5	,,	317	1932	561	T.3–5	,,	378	1930
582	X.2–6	3/91	319	1931	562	T.3–6	,,	379	1931
583	X.2–7	4/91	320	,,	563	T.3–7	,,	380	1945
584	X.2–8	,,	321	1933	564	T.3–8	4/93	381	1931
585	X.2–9	5/91	322	1931	565	T.3–9	,,	382	1933
586	X.2–10	,,	323	1942	566	T.3–10	5/93	383	1931
587	F.3–1	10/91	335	1937	567	S.5–1	,,	384	1933
588	F.3–2	11/91	336	1932	568	S.5–2	,,	385	1932
589	F.3–3	,,	337	1931	569	S.5–3	6/93	386	,,
590	F.3–4	12/91	340	1937	570	S.5–4	,,	387	1931
591	F.3–5	,,	343	1932	571	S.5–5	,,	388	1943
592	F.3–6	3/92	346	1936	572	S.5–6	8/93	389	1931
593	F.3–7	,,	348	1931	573	S.5–7	9/93	390	,,
594	F.3–8	,,	349	,,	574	S.5–8	10/93	392	1933
595	F.3–9	4/92	350	1930	575	S.5–9	,,	393	1932
596	F.3–10	5/92	352	1931	576	S.5–10	11/93	397	1933
677	T.6–1	9/95	460	1933	657	X.6–1	12/95	467	1940
678	T.6–2	10/95	463	1936	658	X.6–2	,,	469	1946
679	T.6–3	11/95	466	1937	659	X.6–3	,,	471	1943
680	T.6–4	12/95	468	,,	660	X.6–4	,,	473	1936
681	T.6–5	,,	470	1943	661	X.6–5	,,	474	,,
682	T.6–6	,,	472	1936	662	X.6–6	,,	475	1933
683	T.6–7	3/96	476	1933	663	X.6–7	5/96	478	1936
684	T.6–8	,,	477	1940	664	X.6–8	,,	480	1943
685	T.6–9	5/96	479	1936	665	X.6–9	6/96	482	1933
686	T.6–10	,,	481	,,	666	X.6–10	,,	483	1943

The following scrap dates (bracketed) may be compared with the withdrawal dates listed in the numerical table. **X2 Nos 581** (9/33), **582** (1/32), **587** (9/38), **590** (3/38), **591** (7/32), **592** (7/37), **593** (2/32), **595** (6/31), **596** (7/32). **T3 558** (1/33), **561** (10/31), **564** (3/32), **569** (2/23), **570** (3/32), **572** and **573** (4/32). The X6s invariably stood several months condemned, e.g., **665** scrapped 1934, **660** and **663** 1937, **661** 1938, **659** and **664** 1944.

Nos 658 (X6), **586** (X2) and **563** (T3) were withdrawn 3/39, and reinstated 4/39.

Longest service, T3 **563,** 52 years; **X2 586** and **X6 658,** 51 years each; T3 **571,** 50 years.

No 657, X6, on being withdrawn in 1940, was used as a stationary boiler until 1943, when it was cut up.

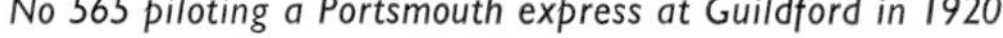

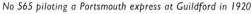

No 565 piloting a Portsmouth express at Guildford in 1920

The following engines were fitted with Drummond boilers at the dates shown. Not all of these were carried at any one time, there being a certain amount of interchange at later periods. when some of the engines reverted to Adams boilers, 558 (1926), 567 (1926), 568 (1907), 583 (1909), 593 (1908), 595 (1926), 658 (1907), 680 (1925), 684 (1932).

All of the class eventually received Drummond chimneys, the last to retain the Adams stovepipes being 566 (until 1920), 580 (1920), 586 (1918), 660 (1924), 663 (1922), 664 (1924), 666 (1920), 679 (1929), 680 (1921), 681 (1928) 684 (1927) and 685 (1926).

The brass beading around the splashers was ultimately removed from all of the engines with the exception of 678, which retained it until the end.

8ft Single 4–2–2

Designed 1893, but not built

The invention of the steam-sanding gear led to a pronounced British revival of the already obsolescent single-wheeler, and it is a matter of historical interest that even so traditionally a 'coupled' line like the LSWR contemplated resurrecting the type.

No single-wheeler had been built for the South Western for more than 33 years when Adams produced a design for a 4–2–2 express engine with 19in × 26in cylinders and 8ft driving wheels. A very fine coloured scale drawing of the projected engine, dated March 14, 1893, preserved in Eastleigh Museum and reproduced herewith, shows a design directly adapted from the existing 7ft 4–4–0s already described.

The drawing is dimensioned as follows. Wheel diameter, bogie 3ft 9$\frac{3}{4}$in driving 8ft 0in, trailing 4ft 10in, the latter an abnormally large idle wheel, and moreover fitted with inside bearings, whereas the contemporary 'Jubilee' 0–4–2s, all had outside bearings. Wheelbase, engine 7ft 6in + 7ft 8in + 8ft 9in, total 23ft 11in; tender 13ft, total (E & T) 45ft 2$\frac{1}{8}$in. Over buffers, 54ft 7$\frac{3}{8}$in. Working pressure, 175lb, boiler pitch 8ft 4in, by far the highest on the system at the time.

The estimated heating surface was greater than the actual hs realised in the 7ft 4–4–0s, viz., tubes 1,264·3sq ft, firebox 126·4sq ft, total 1,390·7sq ft, and the grate area 19·75sq ft would have been precisely that realised in the T3s, which had the largest grate of any Adams engine.

The estimated weight in working order was 50 tons 0cwt, distributed 18 tons 10cwt + 19 tons 0cwt + 12 tons 10cwt, total with the standard 3,500 gallon tender, previously described, 83 tons 4cwt.

This interesting engine was not built. Not only was Adams essentially a 'coupled' man, but he must have realised that such a machine would be very restricted in its scope on a line like the South Western, the conditions of which had forced the elder Beattie to discard single driving wheels as far back as 1859.

All the same, one would very much have liked to see a few of these engines, no doubt they would have found a useful sphere of activity in working the semi-fasts between Basingstoke and Waterloo, for which they would have been quite suitable.

Instead of proceeding with the 4–2–2, for which no running number appears on the drawing, Adams produced Class X6 and it was left to Drummond to break the 'coupled' tradition with his 4–2–4T inspection cab, the small motor-train 2–2–0Ts, and if they can be accepted as 'single-wheelers', his 4–2–2–0s.

Engineer's Department Locomotives

A sizeable stock had been assembled by Engineer's (Permanent Way) Dept., for ballasting and similar work, of which some had been bought new, and others had been transferred from the Running Department. These engines were known by names only in the ED list, but, as from 1887, they were given a new series of numbers, 01–015—the ED list. The complete ED list, so far as it affects our period, is as follows:

The history of *Scott* is sufficiently interesting to warrant extended mention. Exhibited in 1862 at the Hyde Park Exhibition, the engine was bought by the Somerset & Dorset Joint Railway, who are said to have adopted the familiar blue livery because a number of their engines came from George England's works, ready-painted in that firm's standard blue colour. The principal duty of this engine, while on the SDJR was to work the Wells branch.

Sold to the LSWR in 1871, SDJ No 11 was transferred to Engineer's Dept., and named after Archibald Scott, General Manager, LSWR. In the course of rebuilding, completed 12/87, the engine was fitted with a new boiler, the tanks were modified to conform to more usual practice, the cylinder diameter was increased to 11¼in, and the respective wheel diameters were increased to 3ft 0in, and 4ft 0in, presumably by the use of thicker tyres. In 1895, the engine was renumbered 015 in the ED list, but in 1898 it went back to capital stock as No 21 and in 1904 it was placed on the duplicate list as 021, indicated by the number on the tank sides being underlined viz. [21].

Scott had a 10ft 0in wheelbase, (4ft 6in + 5ft 6in) working pressure 120lb, over buffers 22ft 8in and weighed 17 tons (5 tons 13cwt + 5 tons 14cwt + 5 tons 13cwt). With No 392 (late *Lady Portsmouth*), detailed below, *Scott* was working on loan to the Lee-on-the-Solent Light Railway in 1903 and for some time after.

The practice of allocating specific locomotives to Engineering and other Departmental duties fell into disuse after 1898, and was not revived until Maunsell's days after the formation of the SR. Thereafter a number of engines was transferred to what was then known as the Service Department and given numbers in its list of all kinds of miscellaneous vehicles, from breakdown cranes and vans to water carriers and the like, very few numbers being in fact allocated to locomotives. The only LSWR engines involved were the inspection engine 'The Bug', No 733 which became No 58S in 1924, the small 0–4–0T

Original No	ED Name	New Rg List No	Type	Date	Builder	Cylinders (in)	Wheel diams	To ED	Sc or *Wdn	Note
—	*Hawkshaw* ...	01	2–4–0	3/57	Geo. England & Co....	14 × 18	3′ 0″ 5′ 0″	NR	6/89	(a)
147 *Isis*	*Brunel* ...	02	,,	3/63	,, ...	16 × 20	3′ 6″ 5′ 0″	3/83	10/89	(b)
148 *Colne*	*Stephenson* ...	03	,,	11/63	,, ...	,,	,,	3/84	4/91	(c)
—	*Locke* ...	04	,,	12/60	,, ...	15 × 18	3′ 0″ 5′ 0″	1862	10/89	(d)
—	*Smeaton* ...	05	,,	12/60 12/88†	,, ...	,,	,,	,,	1/92	(e)
—	*Telford* ...	06	,,	3/61	,, ...	,,	,,	NR	2/93	(f)
—	*Fowler* ...	07	,,	,,	,, ...	16 × 18	3′ 6″ 5′ 0″	1881	6/90	(g), (h)
—	*Mina* ...	08	0–4–0ST	1872 8/82†	J. Walker, Wigan ...	Outside 10 × 16	2′ 9″	1884	*3/92	(m)
201	*Harrison* ...	09	2–4–0	1862 12/82†	Geo. England & Co.	16 × 18	3′ 0″ 5′ 0″	12/72	6/89	(f)
202	*Bidder* ...	010	,,	1862 12/72†	,,	,,	,,	,,	,,	—
229	*Yolland* ...	011	0–6–0	3/66	R. Stephenson & Co. (1670) ...	16 × 24	5′ 0″	6/75	,,	(f)
230	*Tyler* ...	012	,,	,,	R. Stephenson & Co. (1686) ...	,,	,,	,,	,,	—
227	*Rich* ...	013	2–4–0	4/66	R. Stephenson & Co. (1668) ...	16 × 22	3′ 6″ 6′ 0″	6/76	12/93	(h), (j)
228	*Hutchinson* ...	014	,,	5/66	R. Stephenson & Co. (1669) ...	,,	,,	6/77	6/77	(j)
—	*Scott* ...	015 21	2–4–0T	12/61 12/87†	Geo. England & Co.	Outside $8\frac{1}{2} \times 11\frac{1}{4}$	2′ $10\frac{1}{2}$″ 3′ 10″	1871	4/09	(k)
—	*Hesketh* ...	NR	2–4–0	1862	,,	16 × 18	5′ 0″	NR	NR	—

(*a*) Geo. England & Co., Hatcham Iron Works, Pomeroy St., New Cross. Works buildings still exist.
(*b*) SDJR Nos 11, 11a, *Isis*, bought by LSWR 1880, renamed on transfer to ED.
(*c*) SDJR Nos 12, 12a, *Colne*, bought by LSWR 1880, renamed on transfer to ED.
(*d*) New boiler, 12/86.
(*e*) Bought by LSWR 1862.
(*f*) Relegated to stationary duty, Nine Elms.
(*g*) SDJR No 14, bought by LSWR 1881.
(*h*) Relegated to stationary duty, Eastleigh carriage works.
(*j*) Ex-passenger engine.
(*k*) SDJR No 11, 1863–71. See further particulars below.
(*m*) Built for Widnes Alkali Co. Bought by LSWR from a Mr Phillips, Newport.

* Date withdrawn.
† Rebuilt.
Sc—Scrapped.
NR—No record.
Wdn—Withdrawn.
Hawkshaw was transferred to Loco. Dept., 1888.

No 0745, which took over duties as shunter at Redbridge sleeper depot in 1927 with the number 77S, and very much later, in BR days, G6 0–6–0T No 238, which was sent in 1950 to Meldon Quarries, from which most of the ballast for SR track was obtained, under the number DS3152. It was replaced in 1960 by another of the same class, No 272, which became DS 682. Also there was Adams Jubilee No 612, withdrawn in 1946 and in use as a stationing boiler as DS3191 until 1951.

Miscellaneous Locomotives

The LSWR acquired a number of odd engines from various sources, particularly during the later years of the Adams régime, and this is a suitable stage in the chronological history to give some particulars of them before passing on to Drummond's days.

The following engines were miscellaneous purchases allocated to the Running Dept:

392 *Lady Portsmouth*, 0–6–0ST, Manning, Wardle, 1862 (Works No 50), bought in 1879 from R. T. Relf, Contractor, Okehampton. Cylinders 12 × 18in, wheel diameter 3ft 0in, wheelbase 10ft 3in (5ft 5in + 4ft 10in), working pressure 120lb, over buffers 21ft 6in, weight (wo) 16 tons 4cwt (5 tons 5cwt + 5 tons 13cwt + 5 tons 6cwt). The name-plate was removed 29/11/89. This was one of the last engines at work with the very ancient type of fluted cast-iron safety-valve casing. Replaced 1902 by a Drummond K10, the engine worked some years beyond, and was on loan with *Scott* to the Lee-on-the-Solent Light Railway in 1903. It was eventually sold out of service in 1913 and passed through various ownerships, being last heard of in 1933.

407 *Pioneer*, 0–4–0ST, Manning, Wardle, 1876 (Works No 594), bought from Relf 9/81 for shunting at Plymouth. Outside cylinders 9 × 13in, wheel diameter 2ft 9in, wheelbase 4ft 9¼in. Sometime temporary shunter at Waterloo end of Waterloo & City 'tube' pending arrival of electric locomotive for the purpose. In 1902, No 407 was in use as a tipping engine on the Woking and Basingstoke widening works. As No 0407, it lay in Eastleigh scrap yard, 1919 and was scrapped in 1921.

408 *Jessie*, companion engine to *Pioneer*, Manning, Wardle, 1876 (Works No 628), bought from Relf with No 407, and for same purpose. Scrapped 6/92.

457 *St. Michael*, similar engine to Nos 407/8 (above), Manning, Wardle, 1871 (Works No 379), bought from Relf 3/83 for use in Lydford area. Available dimensions as quoted under No 407. Re-sold to Relf, 6/93 for work on new lines in Plymouth area, possibly the Admiralty railways at Devonport.

458 *Jumbo*, 0–6–0ST, apparently similar to No 392 (above). Said to have been built by Manning, Wardle, 1862, but not traceable in builders' records. Bought 9/83 from J. T. Chappell, named *Steyning* and painted LBSCR yellow livery, from which the supposition that it was used by contractors for the LBSCR, possibly T. Savin or Peto & Betts. Dimensions are reported identical with those of No 392. Worked Bodmin-Wadebridge service from 6/86 to 6/95, scrapped 6/96.

459 *Sambo*, similar to *Jumbo*, and equally non-traceable in Manning, Wardle's list. Rebuilt 1882, bought 1/84 from Chappell, nameplate removed 24/5/90, vacuum brake control fitted 5/90. Some reports give the engine as scrapped 6/97, others as sold at that date.

— *Bodmin*, four-coupled saddle tank, Fletcher, Jennings, Whitehaven, 1863. Cylinders 12 × 20in, wheel diameter 4ft 0in. Worked on Bodmin-Wadebridge line. Scrapped 7/93.

In 1892, the LSWR absorbed the Southampton Dock Company, and its engines were ultimately transferred, for statistical purposes, to the Running List. The engines concerned were all outside-cylinder 0–4–0ST:

Canute, Dick & Stephenson, Airdrie, cylinders 10 × 20in, wheel diameter 3ft 0in. Sold 1896.

Smeaton, *built in 1860 and bought by the LSWR in 1862 for the Engineer's Department, later becoming No 05 in the ED list. Scrapped 1892*

Scott, *here after transfer to the Engineer's Department*

No 0111 Vulcan *at Eastleigh in* 1922

Sir Bevis, *Ascupart*, *Arbroath*, Shanks, Arbroath, all with outside cylinders 10 × 20in, wheel diameter 3ft 0in, all sold 1893.

118 *Vulcan*, Vulcan Foundry, 1878 (Works No 836), cylinders and wheels of above dimensions, wheelbase variously recorded 5ft 0in, or 5ft 6in, working pressure 120lb, tank capacity 350 gallons, weight (wo) about 17½ tons. The number 118 was allotted on acquisition of the Dock Co's stock. Renumbered 111 (12/99), 0111 (1904). Sold 1924.

408 *Bretwalda*, identical with *Vulcan* (above). Vulcan Works No 837. Not numbered in LSWR List until 1900. Renumbered 0408 (1906). Withdrawn 1924, sold to J. Wood, Southampton, 1926, scrapped by them, 1935.

457 *Clausentum*, Hawthorn, Leslie, 1890 (Works No 2174). Cylinders 12 × 20in, wheel diameter 3ft 0in, afterwards 3ft 2in, wheelbase 5ft 6in, working pressure 120lb, tank capacity NR, weight (wo) variously stated 18 tons 10cwt (possibly the 'mean weight'), 21 tons 2cwt. Received number 457, in 1901. Transferred 3/01 to Running Dept. for working Southampton Town Quay and Pier, replaced in Docks list by Adams B4 No 89 *Trouville*. Renumbered 0457 (7/13), 734 (1920). Withdrawn 9/45.

458 *Ironside*, dimensions identical with No 457 (above). Hawthorn, Leslie, 1890 (Works No 2175). Received number 458, 1901. Transferred to Running Dept. with No 457 for purpose stated above; replaced in Docks list by Adams B4 No 90 *Caen*. Renumbered 0458 (12/13), 3458 (11/31), and BRs No 30458. *Ironside*, the last survivor of the Southampton Dock Co's engine stock, was for a time, shed pilot at Guildford. It was scrapped in 1954.

Nos **457** and **458** were ultimately granted status as 0458 Class.

The following engines were 0–4–0ST of Shanks' *Sir Bevis* class bought by LSWR for working along Southampton Town Quay and Pier:

108 *Cowes*, built 11/77, cylinder and wheel dimensions as given under heading *Sir Bevis*, etc. (above). Wheelbase, 5ft 6in, working pressure 120lb, over buffers 21ft 3in, weight (wo) 18 tons 7½cwt. Received number 108, in 1898, in the form of individual brass numerals of Adams type. Renumbered 0108 (1904). Sold 1915 to Plenmellor Colliery, Haltwhistle.

109 *Southampton*, built 12/76, identical with *Cowes* (above). Fitted with vacuum brake control, 7/89. Sold 1915 to Kynochs, Longparish.

110 *Ritzebuttel*, built 6/79 for Southampton Dock, bought by LSWR from that company 12/79. Dimensions as given under No 108 (above). Fitted with vacuum brake control, 6/90. Sold 1916 to Kynochs, Birmingham. The name of this engine was that of an outlying district of Hamburg.

The Shanks engines were all condensing, and had solid cast-iron disc wheels, and connecting rods of circular section. The exhaust steam pipes of Nos 108, 109 entered the saddle tank with a bend nearly as high as the chimney. The cylinders were in all cases horizontal.

734, 735 (afterwards granted status as 735 Class) were two Stroudley A-class 'Terrier' 0–6–0 tank engines bought 3/03 from the LBSCR in readiness for working the Axminster-Lyme Regis branch, which was opened 24/8/03. Cylinders, (No 735) 13 × 20in, (No 734) 14 × 20in, wheel diameter 4ft 0in, wheelbase 12ft 0in, equally divided, working pressure 140lb, tank capacity 500 gallons, over buffers 26ft 0½in, weight (wo) 26 tons 17cwt. The two engines were not repainted by LSWR until some weeks after their arrival at Nine Elms.

No 734 was LBSCR 646, originally 46 *Newington*, built at Brighton, 12/76, put into traffic, 1/77. It was fitted with Drummond boiler, 1912, and sold, 6/13, to the Freshwater, Yarmouth and Newport Railway, who were about to work their own services following disagreement with the Isle of Wight Central Railway. The engine worked for some time on the FYNR in LSWR livery, afterwards became FYNR No 2 livery blue. Absorbed into SR stock, the

Old Manning Wardle saddle tank No 0407

The earliest railway to become part of the LSWR was the Bodmin & Wadebridge, remote in West Cornwall, and for many years isolated from any other line. Opened in 1834, and leased to the LSWR in 1845, it was not until 1895 that the main system finally linked with its old outpost at Wadebridge. When B&Ws only locomotive Bodmin, required heavy repairs, the LSWR had to provide a substitute; before the rail connection, it had to be shipped by sea to Wadebridge

Stroudley Terrier, one of two engines purchased from the LB&SCR in 1903

No 734 Clausentum *at Eastleigh in 1928*

engine successively became No W2, W2 *Freshwater*, W8 *Freshwater*, and was rebuilt at Ryde Works with extended smokebox and bunker. It returned to the mainland as BR 32646, and on withdrawal was restored to LBSC yellow livery as No 46 *Newington* and now does duty as a public house sign outside a hostelry on Hayling Island.

No 735 was LBSCR 668, originally 68 *Clapham*, built at Brighton and put into traffic 8/74. It was fitted with Drummond boiler, 1912, and in 1920 received a 'stove-pipe' chimney barrel of the Adams pattern. At the time, No. 735 was working a pull-and-push unit on the Lee-on-the-Solent branch (which the LSWR had taken over).

The above duty was the last regular passenger work of this engine, and after some years at Ashford Works, No 735 was withdrawn in 1936, with 62 years' service to its credit.

The next two classes to be described bridge the period between the end of Adams' superintendency and the beginning of the Drummond régime, in that although designed by Adams they were perpetuated by Drummond with only slight modifications, whereas his other designs were completely new in concept.

No 108 Cowes, *one of the miscellaneous Southampton Docks shunters*

No 100 was one of the Adams built engines

B4 & K14 Classes Dock Shunting 0–4–0T

Total in classes: 25. Built: LSWR 1891–3 and 1908

In 1891, Adams introduced his standard four-wheeled dock shunting engine, of which Nine Elms built 20, Class B4 between October, 1891 and the end of 1893, and another five in 1908, Class K14, slightly smaller and with variations due to Drummond. The two classes were uniformly coded as 'B4.'

The principal features of these useful engines are outside cylinders with inside valve gear, extremely short wheelbase, and a small coal bunker inside the footplate, close to the firebox back plate. They were not classed for power.

The principal dimensions common to both the Adams and the Drummond lots are as follows: Outside cylinders, 16in × 22in. Wheel diameter, 3ft 9¾in, wheelbase, 7ft 0in. Working pressure, 140lb per sq in, boiler pitch 5ft 10in above rail, outside firebox 3ft 9in long, grate area 10·78sq ft, tank capacity 600 gallons, coal 10cwt. The tube diameter 1¾in, tube length 7ft 10in, and length of boiler barrel (which was a single plate) from tube plate to throat plate, 10ft 8in, were uniform throughout, and the important differences in dimensions may be compared as follows:

	Adams, B4	*Drummond H41*
Height over chimney	12ft 0in	11ft 5 9/16in
Boiler barrel, external diameter	3ft 9in	3ft 8in
Tubes (1¾in)	152	142
Heating surface (sq ft):		
Tubes	766	709
Firebox	57	55
Total	823	764
Front overhang	8ft 0¾in	8ft 1¼in
Rear overhang	9ft 9¾in	9ft 10¼in
Over buffers	24ft 10½in	24ft 11½in
Weight on leading axle	15 tons 0cwt	14 tons 13cwt
Weight on driving axle	18 tons 9cwt	18 tons 5cwt
Total weight (wo)	33 tons 9cwt	32 tons 18cwt

At an early date, some of the Adams lot were sent to Southampton Docks which the LSWR had recently taken over from the Southampton Dock Company, and to suit the restricted headroom and lookout, the enclosed cabs were altered to a canopy which was still in evidence in SR days, though it was being superseded as occasion offered.

The engines allocated to the Running Dept. were fitted with the standard Adams cab No 100, and to this design the later Drummond engines conformed, with the especial difference among others, that the Drummond boiler had its dome mounted close to the firebox. There was also the minor difference that the Drummond frames had a slot cut out to reduce their weight. Two engines of this lot also went to Southampton Docks, and the complete list of transfer dates is therefore as follows:

No	*Name*	*Date*	*No*	*Name*	*Date*	*No*	*Name*	*Date*
81	*Jersey* ...	1893	93	*St. Malo* ...	1896	102	*Granville* ...	1896
85	*Alderney* ...	1900	95	*Honfleur* ...	,,	176	*Guernsey* ...	1893
86	*Havre* ...	1896	96	*Normandy* ...	1893	746	*Dinan* ...	1908
89	*Trouville* ...	1901	97	*Brittany* ...	,,	747	*Dinard* ...	,,
90	*Caen* ...	,,	98	*Cherbourg* ...	1900			

The policy of naming the above engines was adopted by the Docks Superintendent, who based it, no doubt, on a long-standing tradition dating from the old Dock Company. The B4 engines so allocated were at first painted invisible green, while engines allocated to the Running Department were at first painted in the passenger livery, and had the Adams number plates fixed centrally on the side tanks, and Nos 91 and 92 were noted thus at Exeter in 1897, where they were employed as station pilots. Those built after 1893, appeared in the dark green goods livery, and the cast-brass number plates were ultimately superseded by transfer numerals (surmounted, however, by the contraction 'No'—the only LSWR engines so distinguished) on the forward cab-side.

A feature of the Docks engines in recent years was the Filtrator, which is seen alongside the dome in the more modern illustrations. This is an apparatus whereby a linseed colloid is continuously infused into the boiler water, so that

No 93 Caen *was one of 14 engines built specially for shunting in Southampton Docks, which the LSWR acquired in 1891. Unusually for this period they were given names, all of Continental origin. Behind the dome is a filtrator, intended to prevent the formation of scale in the boiler*

St. Malo in Southampton Docks shed in 1936;

by 1954 it was BR No 30093, shunting at Poole Harbour

the salts normally present in the water are deposited in the form of a soft sludge which can be readily washed out.

It is curious that none of the B4 engines was built with a power brake, though most, if not all, were originally fitted with vacuum brake ejectors. The earlier engines transferred to Southampton had the ejectors removed, and worked with hand brakes only, but in after years the vacuum control was restored.

In the official list, dated 1/1/31, six B4s are entered as having hand brake only, Nos 85/6, 95/6, 102, 176, and the rest are listed as 'Hand Brake with Vacuum Ejector'.

Works No	*Date*	*Nine Elms Works No*	*Wdn*	*No*	*Works No*	*Date*	*Nine Elms Works No*	*Wdn*	*No*	*Works No*	*Date*	*Nine Elms Works No*	*Wdn*
D.6–1	11/93	394	1949	90	B.4–6	11/92	368	1948	99	D.6–7	12/93	402	1949
K.14–3	6/08	815	1957	91	B.4–7	,,	370	1948	100	D.6–8	,,	403	1949
K.14–4	,,	816	1959	92	B.4–8	12/92	372	1949	102	D.6–9	,,	406	1963
K.14–5	,,	817	1959	93	B.4–9	,,	374	1960	103	D.6–10	,,	407	1949
B.4–1	10/91	334	1949	94	B.4–10	,,	376	1957	176	D.6–2	10/93	391	1948
B.4–2	12/91	344	1959	95	D.6–3	11/93	395	1949	746 }	K.14–1	4 /08	809	1948
B.4–3	,,	345	1958	96	D.6–4	,,	396	1963	101 }				
B.4–4	10/92	363	1959	97	D.6–5	,,	398	1949	747 }	K.14–2	,,	811	1949
B.4–5	11/92	366	1963	98	D.6–6	,,	398	1949	147 }				

Nos 82/3/4 were the last engines built at Nine Elms Works.
Nos 746/7 renumbered as shown 2/22.

Some of the engines were sold out of service to various industrial firms, and at least one of them, No 30096 (BR number) was still at work in the Southampton area in 1968, under the name *Corrall Queen*. Efforts are now being made towards its preservation. No 30102 was purchased by Sir Billy Butlin and is on view at his holiday camp at Ayr, in Scotland.

The Drummond-built engines, Nos 82–84, 101 and 147 in later years, exchanged boilers with some of the Adams ones.

All the Adams engines eventually received Drummond chimneys, although some of them, surprisingly late compared with other classes. The last ones so fitted were No 94 (until at least 1936), 100 (1945) and 103 (1946).

Adams standard shunting tank was of the usual 0–6–0T variety, and as the class was perpetuated by Drummond without alteration apart from the substitution of his own design of chimney, we can anticipate the later regime by dealing with the whole class here. In all, 34 engines were built between 1894 and 1900. No 257, the first G6, as originally built

G6 & M9 Classes Goods 0–6–0T

Total in classes: 34. Built: LSWR 1894–1900

For shunting and short goods traffic, Adams commenced a series of six-coupled tank engines, Class G6, in 1894, which Drummond increased to a grand total of 34, all built at Nine Elms.

Twelve years had passed since Adams built the previous 0–6–0STs, and those had been merely additions to an existing Beyer, Peacock design adopted by his predecessor, so that, properly speaking, the new G6 engines were really Adams' first and only 0–6–0Ts.

No E272, built after Drummond had taken over, also started with a stovepipe chimney, but later acquired the Drummond pattern. Rather oddly, it reverted to stovepipe for a time. Exmouth Junction, 1924

Again, although none was built with Drummond type boiler, a number acquired them subsequently, as 267 at Exmouth Junction in 1936

The G6s were in many respects duplicates of the O2 bogie tanks with requisite alterations to suit the six-coupled wheels, which were of the same diameter as the O2 driving wheels (4ft 10in). The cylinders were of the later O2 dimensions, 17½in × 24in, and the O2 dimensions relative to boiler barrel, firebox, heating surfaces, grate area, etc., apply here.

Dimensions appropriate to Class G6 include the following. Wheelbase 6ft 10in + 7ft 5in, total 14ft 3in. Length over buffers, 30ft 8½in, tank capacity 1,000 gallons, weight (wo), 47 tons 1cwt.

Adams retired during the production of Class G6, and the later examples displayed slight Drummond influences such as smooth number plates, but underwent no important alterations. Having thus brought the total to 20 units, Drummond found the class so useful that he added 10 more engines with variations of his own, including the Drummond chimney, although the retained the Adams design of boiler.

This extension lot was at first classed M9, but was later embodied in the general classification, G6. The most important difference was a reduction of tubular heating surface to 853sq ft, which may have been accountable to fewer tubes as well as to the shorter M9 barrel, 8ft 10½in, against 9ft 5in. The firebox heating surface was increased to 94sq ft, but the total hs, 947sq ft was 40·5sq ft less than the G6 total. The grate was larger than that of the G6, area 14·8sq ft, against 13·83sq ft, and the total weight of the engine (wo) was 46 tons 15cwt.

The above difference in boiler dimensions is explained by the fact that Drummond had on hand a number of spare boilers intended for further rebuilding of the Beattie well-tanks, and these he now used, with the consequence

All of the class lasted into BR days although not all received 30000 numbers. No 30277 is seen here at Eastleigh in 1949

that Class M9 displayed Adams boiler mountings, such as Ramsbottom safety-valves and the forward siting of the dome.

With the above exceptions, the G6 dimensions are applicable to the M9s. They were built with hand brakes and vacuum ejectors, and the provision of vacuum brake complete is of comparatively recent date. At 1/1/31, only a dozen were thus fitted, Nos 237/8/9, 257/9, 263/7, 270/5/6/7/8, the rest being done by November, 1947. All were unclassed for power.

The principal duty of Class G6 as a whole was in the shunting yards, for which purpose the engines were fitted with heavier buffer beams and a shunter's footboard and handrail abreast the bunker side. A few were employed in banking trains up the 48 chains at 1 in 37 between Exeter St. David's and Exeter Central before the E1/R 0–6–2Ts displaced them, and the others were distributed to various freight centres, with a preponderating number at Nine Elms.

Order No	*Date*	*Nine Elms Works No*	*Wdn*	*No*	*Order No*	*Date*	*Nine Elms Works No*	*Wdn*	*No*	*Order No*	*Date*	*Nine Elms Works No*	*Wdn*
M.9–1	3/00	585	1959	263	G.6–7	10/94	430	1949	274	X.7–4	2/98	527	1960
M.9–2	4/00	586	1958	264	G.6–8	,,	431	1949	275	X.7–5	3/98	528	1949
D.9–1	9/98	544	1949	265	G.6–9	,,	432	1949	276	M.9–3	4/00	587	1949
D.9–2	,,	545	1962	266	G.6–10	,,	433	1960	277	M.9–4	,,	588	1961
D.9–3	,,	546	1948	267	C.7–1	11/96	494	1949	278	M.9–5	5/00	589	1948
D.9–4	10/98	548	1949	268	C.7–2	,,	495	1950	279	D.9–5	11/98	549	1948
G.6–1	6/94	419	1949	269	C.7–3	,,	496	1949	348	R.9–1	5/00	590	1948
G.6–2	8/94	423	1961	270	C.7–4	,,	497	1959	349	R.9–2	,,	591	1961
G.6–3	9/94	426	1950	271	X.7–1	12/97	524	1948	351	R.9–3	6/00	592	1949
G.6–4	,,	427	1958	272*	X.7–2	2/98	525	1960	353	R,9–4	,,	593	1951
G.6–5	,,	428	1948	273	X.7–3	,,	526	1949	354	R.9–5	,,	594	1949
G.6–6	,,	429	1949										

Nos 238 and 272 were renumbered in the Departmental list as DS 682 and DS 3152 in 1960 and 1950 ectively.

Although most of the class came out during Drummond's time, they were all fitted with Adams type boilers (mostly from withdrawn Beattie 2–4–0Ts and 2–4–0s). It was not until 1925 that one of them, No 278, received a Drummond type boiler, followed by 240 in 1928 and 349 in 1929. At a later period, from 1935 onwards, others acquired this type from O2 0–4–4Ts in the Isle of Wight, where they were found to be unsatisfactory. The engines involved were Nos 160, 257 to 261, 267, 269, 273, 274, 279, 351 and 354.

The original engines were built with Adams stove pipe chimneys, but those which came out after 1898 had the Drummond type from the start. All the others eventually received them, although curiously enough No 272 reverted to stove-pipe between 1924 and 1928. No 262 also lost its stove pipe in 1928, and the last, Nos 261, 263 and 265, in 1929.

CHAPTER FIVE

THE DRUMMOND ENGINES

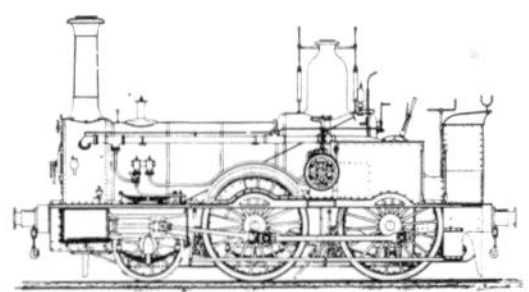

M7 & X14 Classes Passenger 0–4–4T

Total in classes: 105. Built: LSWR 1897-1911

CLASS G6 brings to a close this review of locomotive construction at Nine Elms to the Adams' designs. With 34 built by Gooch, and 209 by the two Beatties, Adams raised the grand total of production at Nine Elms to 497 engines. The 500th was the third of Drummond's M7 bogie tanks, No 244.

During 1896, various orders placed for engines of Adams' designs were completed by Drummond who introduced a few detail differences in external finish, etc., but in the following year the first engines of Drummond's own design appeared, a series of passenger tank engines not unlike Adams' latest in some respects but quite different in others.

For instance, whereas Adams had worked his 0–4–4 tanks at 160lb pressure, Drummond adopted 150lb per sq in (later increased to 175lb). He adhered to the 5ft 7in diameter coupled wheels, but increased the bogie wheel diameter from 3ft 0in to 3ft 7in. The boiler was slightly larger in diameter but 6in shorter; the firebox was, however, 4in longer and sloped so that the forward end was 6in lower than the footplate end, and the grate was correspondingly inclined. Adams, on the other hand, had used a deeper box with a horizontal grate.

Other differences were that the Drummond cylinders were larger, 18½in × 26in, and the reversing lever was on the left-hand side instead of on the right, which had been the standard position from Joseph Beattie's time. Also, the new Drummond engines had their firebox back lagged in Stroudley fashion to keep the cab cool.

The principal dimensions of the M7 engines are as follows: Boiler barrel 4ft 5⅛in minimum outside diameter × 10ft 6in, pitched 7ft 6in centre above rail, pressed at 175lb, and containing 216 tubes, 1¾in outside diameter. Length of firebox 6ft 4in. Wheel diameter, see above. Wheelbase coupled, 7ft 6in, bogie 6ft 6in, total 23ft 7in. Length over buffers 35ft 0¼in, height over chimney 13ft 2⅝in. Water capacity, 1,300 gallons, coal capacity originally 3 tons, but somewhat increased from 1920 onwards by the addition of two extra coal rails to the existing grid of three. Weight (wo), 17 tons 8cwt + 18 tons 0cwt + 24 tons 16cwt, total 60 tons 4cwt. Power class was K.

The first 55 M7 engines were built at Nine Elms between March, 1897, and October, 1900, and there were several external details which marked them as of Drummond origin, viz., the flared-top chimney in place of the Adams severe—but handsome—stovepipe, the direct-loaded safety-valves mounted on the dome a new type of cab and a new type of number plate of the pattern used by Drummond on the Scottish lines with which he had previously been connected. From 1903 onwards this design of number plate was superseded by transfer numerals. Dates of construction were not shown on any of Drummond's engines built in the Company's own works.

No 243, and probably all the 1897 lot, had a conical smokebox door, which was associated with an early experiment in spark arresters. It may have been an attempt at increasing the volume of the smokebox for this purpose, and at this date, it must be remembered, the modern extended smokebox was only just coming into vogue.

When the M7 Class was introduced, the lettering on the tanks was varied. The first batch had 'SWR', the next appeared with 'LSW', and in 1898, it was decided to adopt 'LSWR.' This, by the way, had been Adam's final choice, after some experiment with 'LSWR'. No 667 was the first of the M7s on which the standard legend 'LSWR' appeared.

From 1903 onwards, further engines were put into traffic generally similar to the earlier engines and different in only few particulars of any importance, e.g., the overall length was increased by 1ft 2¾in to 36ft 3in, and they had tubular feed water heaters in the side tanks comprising a total of 40 tubes (11ft 3½in × 2in diameter, total heating surface, 234sq ft) through which the exhaust steam from the cylinders was led. The feed water did not come into direct contact with the exhaust steam and so was kept free from grease and oil which so largely account for over-heating of the firebox plates. There was no alteration to the boiler and firebox dimensions, and the respective capacities of

Drummond 044T No 111 in original condition at Strawberry Hill in 1920. For some unknown reason this engine was always unofficially known as 'Lord Nelson' (this was of course long before the advent of Maunsell's 4-6-0s). The number of coal rails on the bunker was increased eventually from three to five on all the engines in the class

tanks and bunker were as before; all the extra length was absorbed in the increased front overhang. An important difference was this lot had steam reversing gear.

The 50 modified engines were classed, as was usual, by the reference number of the original order for their construction, in this case 'X14', and were built between February, 1903 and November, 1911, the last ten coming from the then newly-established Eastleigh Works. A large majority of this lot were later fitted with pull-and-push gear for auto-train working and engines so equipped weighed 62 tons 0cwt.

In 1921, Urie rebuilt No 126 with an 'Eastleigh' superheater, increased the cylinder diameter to 19in, raised the boiler centre by 9in to 8ft 3in (modifying the cab to suit) and fitted an extended smokebox with his own design of 'stovepipe' chimney. The new boiler was of the type then being used for rebuilding Drummond's 700 Class goods engines; it contained 112 tubes $1\frac{3}{4}$in outside diameter and 18 superheater flues $5\frac{1}{4}$in outside diameter, but its working pressure was set at 170lb. The following table compares No 126 before and after the above rebuilding.

	Before	*After*
Heating Surface (sq ft)—		
Small Tubes	1067·7	593
Large Tubes	—	266·5
Firebox	123·9	117
Total Evaporative	1191·6	976·5
Superheater	—	167
Total Combined	—	1143·5
Working Pressure (lb/sq in)	175	170
Grate Area (sq ft)	20·36	20·36
Weight—Full—		
On coupled wheels	35 tons 5cwt	39 tons 4cwt
On bogie wheels	24 tons 18cwt	23 tons 14cwt
Total	60 tons 3cwt	62 tons 18cwt

To compensate the extra weight at the leading end due to the superheater, a heavy cast-iron balance weight was placed at the opposite end to minimise unsteady running.

At Strawberry Hill in 1923 stands 377, one of the small number which differed from the majority in having the leading sandboxes below the running plate instead of being combined with the leading splashers

No 50 passing Clapham Junction with a heavy train in 1928. Drummond would probably have been annoyed to have seen this sight—he always insisted on engines being fired very economically, visible emission of smoke or even blowing off of safety valves being a serious offence in his eyes

No 481 running round on Lymington Pier in 1928. The pulleys on the cab roof were part of the early type of cable-operated pull and push apparatus, not in use on this occasion

Fitted with more modern air control push and pull apparatus, No 30108 is seen at Wareham in 1960, working, sandwich fashion, with its own two-coach set and with the two through coaches from Waterloo to Swanage

Only one of the class was ever rebuilt, No 126 being provided with a superheater by Urie in 1921. Unsatisfactory, and said to be unsteady at speed, it was scrapped in 1937

Although the superheating of other Drummond classes proved, in the main, markedly advantageous, the altered No 126 was too heavy for many of the suburban lines and it was withdrawn in May, 1937, and dismantled so that its standard parts could be used for maintaining the other M7 engines. The spares thus released included the boiler, which thereupon became suitable for superheater engines of the 700 Class by the simple expedient of raising the working pressure to the 700 Class figure of 180lb.

Incidentally, though No 126 was officially scrapped in August, 1937, the frames were used for No 254, so that it might be said that No 254 was scrapped and the frames of No 126 were renumbered No 254.

The earliest engines were used on fast trains between Exeter and Plymouth, but were relegated to the London suburban traffic after No 252 came off the road at high speed between Brentor and Tavistock on 6/3/98, and rolled over.

No 58 on Thursday, 26/4/23 worked a special train of 3 standard LSWR coaches from Waterloo to Bookham conveying the then Duke and Duchess of York (later King George VI and Queen Elizabeth, now Queen Mother) on the first stage of their honeymoon journey. The engine (in LSWR livery) was meticulously polished but not in anyway adorned, and carried three head-boards, respectively one white at base of chimney, one ditto left hand of smokebox, and one white with a black spot left hand of buffer-beam.

Nos 112/23/4/30/2/3, 318-24, 356/7/74-8 originally had the leading sandboxes situated in the smokebox. They were later placed below the running plate. The leading splashers of these engines were of the plain quadrant profile.

Nos 242-256 when new were fitted with the Caledonian type of hooter, but ordinary whistles were soon substituted.

No 244 (3/97) was the 500th engine built at Nine Elms works, **No 322** (8/00) the 600th, and **No 29** (2/04) the 700th.

As many of these engines were becoming increasingly displaced from their London area suburban duties by extension of electrification, they were drafted to the country areas. Many were fitted with pull and push apparatus. At first it was of the simple cable and pulley type, the first engines so adapted being No 481, in 1912, followed by several others. In 1930 the much more modern and efficient Westinghouse air control system was adopted; eventually some forty-five engines were so fitted.

No	*Order No*	*Date*	*Works No*	*Wdn*
21	B.12–1	1/04	697	1964
22	E.9–1	1/99	554	1958
23	E.9–2	1/99	555	1961
24	E.9–3	1/99	556	1963
25	E.9–4	2/99	557	1964
26	E.9–5	2/99	558	1959
27	B.12–2	1/04	698	1959
28	B.12–3	1/04	699	1962
29	B.12–4	2/04	700	1964
30	B.12–5	2/04	701	1959
31	V.7–1	3/98	529	1963
32	V.7–2	3/98	530	1963
33	V.7–3	4/98	531	1962
34	V.7–4	4/98	532	1963
35	V.7–5	4/98	533	1963
36	V.7–6	5/98	534	1964
37	V.7–7	5/98	535	1958
38	V.7–8	5/98	536	1958
39	V.7–9	5/98	537	1963
40	V.7–10	6/98	538	1961
41	E.9–6	3/99	539	1957
42	E.9–7	3/99	560	1957
43	E.9–8	3/99	561	1961
44	E.9–9	3/99	562	1961
45	X.12–5	5/05	743	1962
46	Y.12–1	5/05	744	1959
47	Y.12–2	5/05	745	1960
48	Y.12–3	5/05	746	1964
49	Y.12–4	5/05	747	1962
50	Y.12–5	6/05	748	1962
51	B.13–1	11/05	751	1962
52	B.13–2	12/05	755	1964
53	B.13–3	12/05	757	*1964
54	B.13–4	12/05	759	1959
55	B.13–5	12/05	761	1963
56	D.13–1	1/06	763	1963
57	D.13–2	1/06	764	1963
58	D.13–3	3/06	765	1960
59	D.13–4	3/06	766	1961
60	D.13–5	3/06	767	1961
104	X.12–1	3/05	739	1961
105	X.12–2	3/05	740	1963
106	X.12–3	3/05	741	1960
107	X.12–4	4/05	742	1964
108	C.12–1	3/04	702	1964
109	C.12–2	3/04	703	1961
110	C.12–3	3/04	704	1963
111	C.12–4	3/04	705	1964
112	B.10–1	7/00	595	1963
123	G.11–1	2/03	665	1959
124	G.11–2	2/03	666	1961
125	X.14–1	8/11	13	1962
126	X.14–2	9/11	14	1937
127	X.14–3	10/11	15	1963
128	X.14–4	11/11	16	1961

No	*Order No*	*Date*	*Works No*	*Wdn*
129	X.14–5	11/11	17	1963
130	G.11–3	2/03	667	1959
131	A.15–1	11/11	18	1962
132	G.11–4	3/03	668	1962
133	G.11–5	3/03	669	1964
241	E.9–10	5/99	564	1963
242	M.7–1	3/97	498	1958
243	M.7–2	3/97	499	1958
244	M.7–3	3/97	500	1957
245	M.7–4	4/97	501	†1962
246	M.7–5	4/97	502	1961
247	M.7–6	4/97	503	1961
248	M.7–7	5/97	504	1961
249	M.7–8	5/97	505	1963
250	M.7–9	5/97	506	1957
251	M.7–10	6/97	507	1963
252	M.7–11	6/77	508	1959
253	M.7–12	6/97	509	1961
254	M.7–13	8/97	511	1964
255	M.7–14	8/97	512	1960
256	M.7–15	8/97	513	1959
318	B.10–2	8/00	596	1959
319	B.10–3	8/00	597	1960
320	B.10–4	8/00	598	1963
321	B.10–5	8/00	599	1962
322	C.10–1	8/00	600	1958
323	C.10–2	10/00	601	1959
324	C.10–3	10/00	602	1959
328	A.15–2	11/11	18	1962
356	C.10–4	10/00	603	1958
357	C.10–5	10/00	604	1961
374	H.11–1	4/03	670	1959
375	H.11–2	5/03	671	1962
376	H.11–3	5/03	672	1959
377	H.11–4	5/03	673	1962
378	H.11–5	5/03	674	1962
379	C.12–5	6/04	713	1963
479	A.15–3	11/11	20	1961
480	A.15–4	12/11	21	1964
481	A.15–5	12/11	22	1959
667	M.7–16	9/97	514	1964
668	M.7–17	9/97	515	1961
669	M.7–18	9/97	516	1961
670	M.7–19	10/97	517	1963
671	M.7–20	10/97	518	1959
672	M.7–21	10/97	519	‡1948
673	M.7–22	11/97	520	1960
674	M.7–23	11/97	521	1961
675	M.7–24	11/97	522	1958
676	M.7–25	11/97	523	1961

* No 53 preserved at Steamtown Museum, U.S.A.
† No 245 retained by BR for preservation.
‡ Scrapped 5/48 after falling down Waterloo and City 'tube' lift shaft at Waterloo.

Works Nos 13–22 indicate built at Eastleigh, all others are Nine Elms Works Nos.

These long lived engines were remarkable in that with the exception of No 126 they remained almost unaltered throughout the whole of their existence, apart from inevitable changes of livery and lettering under three ownerships. Even the design of the chimney remained the same, itself unusual as successive locomotive designers usually had their own ideas on this subject. The Drummond tanks could be seen partaking in a small way on what amounts to a main line duty right into the early 1960s, when they could be seen valiantly working the main portion of eight coaches or so from Bournemouth West to Bournemouth Central, where they joined up with the Weymouth portion, probably only a three coach set, which had been brought in by a Pacific to continue to Waterloo.

No 691 as originally built with the conical smokebox door

700 Class Goods 0–6–0

Total in class: 30. Built: Dübs 1897

As Nine Elms Works were fully occupied, Drummond placed an order with Dübs, Glasgow, for 30 0–6–0 goods engines, which were delivered while the first batch of M7 tanks was being completed. Ten years had elapsed since any 0–6–0 tender engines had been added to the LSWR stock, and after the 700 Class appeared, no more of this wheel arrangement were found necessary. This is hardly surprising in view of the success of Adams' 0–4–2 'Jubilees', which were handy for either passenger or freight traffic.

The new Dübs goods engines had boilers which were exact duplicates of, and interchangeable with, those of the M7s, but since the coupled wheels were 6in smaller, the boiler centre was pitched 3in lower, bringing it 7ft 3in above rail, and reducing the height over chimney to 12ft $11\frac{5}{8}$in. The cylinder dimensions

No 352 in SR days, before rebuilding

All were rebuilt by Urie with superheater; this view shows No 316 in early BR style, with the prefix S, before renumbering to 30316

No 30700 piloting a West Country 34012 on a troop train near Medstead & Four Marks in 1955

also were identical with those of the M7s, and, therefore, the figures already given under the above headings need not be repeated.

The remaining dimensions were as follows. Coupled wheels, 5ft 1in diameter, engine wheelbase 16ft 6in (7ft 6in + 9ft 0in). Tender on six wheels, 4ft 0in diameter, tender wheelbase 13ft 0in, equally divided. Total wheelbase, E & T, 39ft 1in, length over buffers 52ft 7in. Weight in working order, engine 42 tons 15cwt, tender 36 tons 14cwt, total 79 tons 9cwt. Tender capacity, 3,500 gallons. The power class was C.

These engines bore Nos 687–716, makers' Nos 3510–3539, but in 1898, Nos 702–16 were re-numbered to make room for the new T9 4–4–0s and in 1912, No 459 (late No 716), was again re-numbered to clear the numerical range below No 458 for Drummond's new 4–6–0s under construction and so keep all the 4–6–0s in sequence.

The 700 Class engines were originally lettered 'SWR' on the tenders, and many, if not all of them, had the conical smokebox door, which was secured with 3 screw dogs, disposed at 120 degrees around its circumference.

In 1921, Urie decided to rebuild No 316 with an 'Eastleigh' superheater, and eventually all the class were similarly dealt with, but from 1924 onwards, the superheaters fitted were of the Maunsell type. The boiler was pitched 9in higher, the cylinder diameter was increased to 19in, and the working pressure was raised from 175lb to 180lb. The heating surface was altered as follows: 112 1¾in tubes 593sq ft, 18 5¼in flues, 266·5sq ft, fire box 117sq ft, total evaporative hs 976·5sq ft, superheater hs 167sq ft in the 'Eastleigh' type, 182sq ft in the 'Maunsell' type.

To suit the extended smokebox, the front end was lengthened by 1ft 6in, increasing the overall length by the same amount, and a new and shorter chimney was fitted which raised the overall height to 13ft 2¾in. This chimney was of Urie's 'stovepipe' pattern with a forward draught-deflecting lip, or 'capuchon', which was of late years discarded, leaving the chimney rim smooth.

No	*Works No*	*Date*	*Super-heated*	*Wdn*
687	3510	3/97	6/23 E	1960
688	3511	,,	7/27 M	1957
689	3512	,,	1/23 E	1962
690	3531	,,	2/26 M	1962
691	3514	,,	11/26 M	1961
692	3515	,,	12/26 M	1962
693	3516	,,	4/26 M	1961
694	3517	,,	3/22 E	1961
695	3518	,,	1/26 M	1962
696	3519	,,	9/26 M	1961
697	3520	4/97	9/25 M	1962
698	3521	,,	10/25 M	1962
699	3522	5/97	3/27 M	1961
700	3523	,,	2/23 E	1962
701	3524	,,	3/27 M	1961

No	*Works No*	*Date*	*Super-heated*	*Wdn*
702 } 306	3525	5/97	4/29 M	1962
703 } 308	3526	,,	10/22 E	1961
704 } 309	3527	,,	1/24 M	1962
705 } 315	3538	,,	10/25 M	1962
706 } 317	3529	,,	4/25 M	1961
707 } 325	3530	6/97	9/25 M	1962
708 } 326	3531	,,	7/23 E	1962
709 } 327	3532	,,	2/26 M	1961

No	*Works No*	*Date*	*Super-heated*	*W*
710 } 339	3533	6/97	5/24 E	19
711 } 346	3534	,,	11/23 E	19
712 } 350	3535	,,	3/22 E	19
713 } 352	3536	,,	5/27 M	19
714 } 355	3537	,,	7/29 M	19
715 } 368	3538	,,	11/22 E	19
716 } 459 } 316	3539	,,	11/20 E	19

E—Eastleigh superheater at date given.
M—Maunsell superheater at date given.
Nos 702–716 renumber as shown 5–98.
No 459 again renumbered 316, 1912.
Boilers with 'E' or 'M' type superheater were subsequently interchanged throughout the class.

Although the 0–6–0 type was widely used on other railways (except the Great North of Scotland), these were destined to be the last for the LSWR, as Drummond built no more. Urie never did.

No 720 in its original condition

T7 & E10 Classes Non-coupled Express 4–2–2–0

Total in classes: 6. Built: LSWR 1897 and 1901

Drummond's third South-Western design struck a new note and was, at the time, unique. No 720, the engine concerned, had 4 high-pressure cylinders driving two independent (*i.e.*, not coupled) pairs of driving wheels which could thus be spaced 11ft apart to allow an extra long firebox. The new engine also introduced the massive double-bogie tender of the type nicknamed 'Water Carts', which Peter Drummond also produced on the Highland Railway.

The principal dimensions of Class T7, which comprised only this one engine, No 720, were: Wheel diameter, driving 6ft 7in, bogie and tender 3ft 7in. The engine bogie wheels were 6ft 6in apart, and those of each tender bogie 5ft 6in. The cylinders were originally 16½in × 26in, but the bore was reduced to 15in before the engine was handed over for traffic, and later it was further reduced to 14in; four 16½in cylinders are equivalent in total demand to two 23in × 26in, for which the following boiler dimensions are obviously inadequate. The boiler 4ft 5⅛in × 12ft 0in, in the barrel, pitched 7ft 9in above rail, and pressed at 175lb, contained 271 tubes 1½in diameter giving a heating surface of 1,307sq ft, to which the firebox added 142sq ft. In addition, 195sq ft were obtained from the 72 2¾in water tubes which were laid across the inner firebox thereby connecting the water space on one side with that on the side opposite. The grate area was 27·4sq ft.

The total hs thus realised was 1,664sq ft, and there was a tubular feed-water heater in the tender well comprising 20 tubes, 18ft × 2½in, giving 235·7sq ft of heating surface. Both the firebox water tubes and the feed-water heater became standard equipment.

The inside cylinders drove the leading driving wheels and were controlled by Stephenson link motion; the outside cylinders drove the rear driving wheels through the medium of an extended piston rod bearing on a top slide bar, and were controlled by Joy's valve gear, arranged as on Webb's 3-cylinder LNWR compounds. Both inside and outside motions were controlled as one by a steam reversing gear similar to James Stirling's of the SER and operated by a small lever on the left-hand side of the cab.

The weight of No 720 in working order was 54 tons 11cwt, of which 18 tons

18cwt rested on the fore drivers, and 18 tons 16cwt on those behind, a total of 37 tons 14cwt adhesive.

The weight of the tender (capacity 4,300 gallons) was 48 tons 18cwt. It was the only one of its particular dimensions and the later standard examples were longer but not so high. In 1915, No 720 and No 335, one of Drummond's 4–6–0s, exchanged tenders and for this purpose, the tender ex-335 had its water capacity increased from 4,000 to 4,500 gallons.

The reader will, no doubt, observe the Stroudley influence behind Drummond's inside-framed tenders, which the two Drummonds, both ex-'Brighton' men, may have adopted for the same reason that originally moved Stroudley to put the bearings inside, viz, to enable carrying wheels to be used under the tender when they had worn too far to be safely used under the engine.

No 720 had some good turns of speed to her credit and in March, 1905, was rebuilt with a larger boiler, 4ft 10¾in × 12ft 0in in the barrel, pitched 8ft 6in above rail and containing 247 1¾in tubes. The total heating surface was 1,760sq ft, made up as follows: boiler tubes 1,392sq ft, firebox water tubes 195sq ft, firebox 173sq ft. The grate area, 27·4sq ft, and the working pressure, 175lb, were as before, and the total engine weight rose to 60 tons 1cwt. The

No 720 as rebuilt with a larger boiler, in Wandsworth Cutting, one of the few known views of it at work. Cut up in 1927, it spent most of its time in Nine Elms Shed

Notwithstanding the indifferent success of the prototype engine, five similar locos, Nos 360–373, appeared in 1901 with sundry modifications. Although some improvement on the original they were never very popular and were used only during times of shortage of motive power. They were never provided with larger boilers. An unusual view of No 371 in 1925, working an empty stock train, tender first, at Clapham Junction in 1925

All five were finally withdrawn during 1926/7, and this picture shows Nos 371 and 369 in Eastleigh scrapyard in 1926

No 372 in its final form with SR livery in Eastleigh yard in 1927. Note the additional sandboxes for the rear driving wheels, in front of the cab, to help to equalise the tendency of the back drivers to slip more frequently than the leading pair. They were fitted to all engines except 371 and 720

tender at this period weighed 49 tons full, giving a combined total weight, E&T, 109 tons 1cwt.

In this form No 720 remained in service until April, 1927, when it was condemned. In August, 1897, the month of its appearance on the road, No 720 was painted yellow in Stroudley's celebrated LBSCR style, but was later repainted in Drummond's regulation LSWR green with a chocolate border defined by a wide black band flanked by two white lines to form the panels.

Class E10 comprised five similar engines Nos 369–373, with divided drive, built at Nine Elms 1901, with four cylinders 14in × 27in, to which dimensions the cylinders of the earlier engine had already been modified. There was no alteration in the various wheel diameters, working pressure or grate area, and the boiler barrel and firebox were of the 1897 dimensions, but the total heating surface was 1,690sq ft, made up as follows: 280 barrel tubes, 1½in diameter, 1,344sq ft, 72 2¾in firebox water tubes, 190sq ft, firebox 156sq ft. The double-bogie tender was of the longer and lower type, capacity 4,500 gallons, weight full 49 tons, which, added to the total engine weight of 58 tons 14 cwt, brought the combined total to 107 tons 14cwt. No 373 lost its firebox water tubes in 1913, 371 in 1916, 372 in 1919, 369 and 370 in 1922, and 720 in 1925.

Detail differences in the later lot included Drummond steam sanding, double slide bars and water-tube inspection doors covered with the afterwards familiar rectangular casings at the sides of the outer firebox. No 720 had been built with bogie-wheel splashers of the kind favoured by P. Stirling and R. Billinton, but these were absent from the new lot and were ultimately removed from the prototype engine. A minor distinction was that the tender of No 720 had been lettered 'LSW', whereas the new lot had the tenders inscribed with the standard legend 'LSWR'.

The T7 and E10 engines were very capable at times, though apt rather to sway at high speed when the disturbance phases of the independent moving masses happened to synchronise, and No 370 was recorded by E. L. Ahrons to have worked a train of 170 tons from pass Clapham Junction to pass Andover 62¼ miles in 61¾ minutes, an average speed of over 60mph. Theoretically, it is surprising that these engines did not last so long as the 4–4–0 engines of corresponding dimensions; the higher tractive effort should have been an advantage but the reason for their earlier withdrawal was that their margin of power proved insufficient as loads increased. The two lots of engines here reviewed were latterly stationed at Nine Elms, but it was not uncommon to find most of them laid by, except in the height of the summer traffic. They were in power Class I.

No	*Order No*	*Date*	*Works No*	*Wdn*	*No*	*Order No*	*Date*	*Works No*	*Wdn*
720	T.7–1	8/97	510	1927	371	E.10–3	6/01	619	1926
369	E.10–1	4/01	612	1926	372	E.10–4	,,	620	1927
370	E.10–2	6/01	618	,,	373	E.10–5	7/01	621	,,

Nos 720, 372, and **373** were repainted in SR livery, but the other three were scrapped as LSWR.

C8 Class Passenger 4–4–0

Total in class: 10. Built LSWR 1898

While No 720 was being put through her paces, Drummond put in hand at Nine Elms a series of 2-cylinder 4–4–0s, Nos 290–9, Class C8, which were reminiscent of the 4–4–0 engines he had previously built for the North British Railway, and very much akin to his '66' or 'Carbrook' Class on the Caledonian.

The C8 boiler was identical and interchangeable with the boilers used on the M7 0–4–4Ts and the 700 Class 0–6–0s, and the boiler data already given under those headings equally apply with the single exception that the C8 centre line was pitched 7ft 9in above rail.

Drummond's first design of 4–4–0, similar to his earlier engines for the NBR and Caledonian Railway. No 292 as originally built

No 294 in Yeovil shed in 1926. All these engines were broken up between 1933 and 1938

The remaining dimensions of the new class were as follows: Cylinders $18\frac{1}{2}$in $\times$ 26in. Wheel diameter, bogie 3ft 7in, coupled 6ft 7in. Wheelbase, coupled 9ft 0in, total engine 22ft 3in (6ft 6in + 6ft 9in + 9ft 0in), total engine and tender 45ft 10in. Total length over buffers, 54ft 11in. Weight in working order, engine 46 tons 16cwt, E&T, 87 tons 0cwt. Power Class I.

The tender in question was of the 700 Class design, carried on 6 wheels 4ft diameter, in outside bearings, coal capacity 4 tons, water 3,500 gallons, weight, full, 40 tons 4cwt. The frame length was not altered, but the wheels were spaced to a total wheelbase of 14ft (instead of 13ft) equally divided.

In later years, the C8 engines were coupled to double-bogie inside-bearing tenders of Drummond's standard type, total wheelbase 14ft 6in (5ft 0in + 4ft 6in + 5ft 0in), which increased the combined E&T wheelbase by 1ft to a total of 46ft 10in, and brought the overall length to 56ft 5¼in. These particular 'water carts' held 4,000 gallons and 5 tons of coal, weighed 44 tons 17cwt full, and increased the total E&T weight to 91 tons 13cwt. Both the above varieties of C8 tender were lettered 'LSWR'.

With the withdrawal of the C8 engines, the double-bogie tenders were transferred to Urie's S15 Class 4-6-0s, Nos 504-10, which had yielded up their own (but outside-framed) bogie tenders to the N15/x 4-6-0s converted from ex-LBSCR 4-6-4 tanks.

Nos 290-9 were built with splasher and sandbox combined as a unit, a Stroudley characteristic that Drummond had so far adopted on all his LSWR engines except No 720. The sandboxes were afterwards attached to the frames beneath the running plate and contemporaneously the profile of the driving splashers was smoothed to the plain quadrant outline.

The firebox water tubes, introduced on No 720, were not adopted on Class C8, but they reappeared on Class T9 which was evolved from the C8s. Unlike the T9s, the C8s were not rebuilt to modern standards, and ended their careers largely in their original condition. Their main trouble was shortage of steam through too small a firebox.

No	*Order No*	*Date*	*Works No*	*Wdn*	*No*	*Order No*	*Date*	*Works No*	*Wdn*
290	C.8-1	6/98	539	1933	295	C.8-6	10/98	547	1935
291	C.8-2	,,	540	1935	296	C.8-7	11/98	550	1935
292	C.8-3	,,	541	1936	297	C.8-8	,,	551	1936
293	C.8-4	7/98	542	1935	298	C.8-9	,,	552	1938
294	C.8-5	8/98	543	1933	299	C.8-10	,,	553	1937

It will be noted that No 298, the last C8 withdrawn, completed nearly 40 years' service, and it is also worth remarking that, with very few exceptions (and then only for special reasons), Drummond's engines were cut up direct from capital stock. The original No 298, a Beattie 2-4-0 well tank of 1874, after nearly 50 years in the duplicate list, was still in service until 1962 though the C8 engine which replaced it in 1898 had long since been scrapped.

No 291, on 23/11/98, worked a special train from Windsor through to Dover (LCDR), conveying the Grand Duke and Duchess Serge of Russia.
No 296 (11/98) was the 550th engine built at Nine Elms.

In their last years most of them were divided between Eastleigh, Salisbury and Yeovil sheds; they were rarely seen in London. They were usually to be found on the then local service between Yeovil and Salisbury.

The only modification made to these engines. apart from the provision of eight-wheeled tenders, was in the removal of the sandboxes, previously combined with the leading splasher, to a new position underneath the frames

No 773, the Exhibition engine, the last T9 to be built, seen here in original condition. The number 733 was already carried by the 4–2–4T inspection engine, but as this was then the highest number in the list, why a jump to 773 was made for the T9 is not very clear. It did in fact become 733 many years later to make way for the new King Arthur Class engine which appeared in 1925

T9 Class Express 4–4–0

Total in class: 66. Built: LSWR and Dübs 1899-1901

A development of the previous C8 Class, the T9, was to prove Drummond's most outstanding success. The main improvement was in the provision of a larger firebox and longer coupled wheelbase, and most of them were also fitted with his cross firebox water tubes, distinguished by the rectangular container seen at the side of the firebox. This device became a standard feature of his main line engines, but was subsequently removed by his successor, Urie. In all, 66 engines of this famous class were built between 1899 and 1901, all gave many years of splendid service, the last not being withdrawn until 1963. (The last survivor, No 120, has fortunately been preserved.)

Constructionally, the T9s were divisible into three main groups, as follows: (A) Nos 113–22 and 280–9 (20 engines), with 6-wheel outside-frame tenders of 14ft wheelbase, equally divided. (B) Nos 702–19 and 721–32 (30 engines), identical with Group (A) but with 61 firebox water tubes, $2\frac{3}{4}$in diameter, yielding 165sq ft hs. (C) Nos 300–5/7/10–4/36–8 (15 engines) basically Group (B), but with wider cab and driving splashers to enclose the throw of the coupling rod when passing through its top centre and so obviate the need for separate coupling-rod splashers. The engines of this group had the sandboxes located at first in the smokebox, like the contemporary M7s, and were allotted 4,000-gallon bogie tenders of the kind already described under the C8 heading.

The odd engine No 773 (SR No 733), belonged to Group (B), formed Dübs exhibit at the Glasgow Exhibition, 1901, and was probably built by them for the purpose, after which the LSWR took it over.

The principal dimensions of all three groups were as follows: Cylinders, 18½in × 26in. Wheel diameter, coupled 6ft 7in, bogie 3ft 7in. Boiler barrel, 4ft 5⅛in minimum external diameter, 10ft 6in from tube plate to throat plate, pitched 7ft 9in centre above rail, pressure 175lb. Outside firebox 7ft 4in long, grate area 24sq ft. Wheelbase, bogie 6ft 6in, coupled 10ft, total engine 23ft 3in, total, engine and tender, Groups (A) and (B) 46ft 10in, ditto Group (C) 47ft 10in. Over buffers, Groups (A) and (B) 55ft 11in, Group (C) 57ft 5⅛in. Weight in working order, Group (A), engine 46 tons 4cwt, E&T, 86 tons 8cwt; Group (B), engine, 48 tons 17cwt, of which 17 tons 15cwt and 15 tons 14cwt rested respectively on the leading and the trailing coupled wheels; engine and tender 89 tons 1cwt; ditto Group (C), E&T 93 tons 14cwt a difference of 4 tons 13cwt entirely comprised in the extra weight of the bogie tender, which scaled 44 tons 17cwt full, distributed 23 tons 2cwt + 21 tons 15cwt. By 1923, all the T9s had this kind of tender, but since that date, the 6-wheel tenders have re-appeared through interchange.

A T9 minus water tubes, prior to superheating, and fitted with 4,000-gallon bogie tender scaled 91 tons 1cwt. After superheating the total rose to 96 tons 13cwt.

The T9s were fitted with the vacuum brake and Nos 337–8 had Westinghouse brake control in addition. They are shown still so fitted in the official list dated 111/31, but had lost the equipment by 1936.

The removal of splasher sand boxes was made usually in conjunction with the provision of superheater, but E710 was the only engine to be so altered without being superheated simultaneously

No 715 at Nine Elms in 1921

Nos 113–122 and 280–289 never had the firebox water tubes. No 122, on an up Portsmouth express, enters Guildford in 1925

In 1922, Urie rebuilt No 314 with an 'Eastleigh' superheater, extended smokebox and stovepipe chimney and in the process he brought the boiler feed clacks to the side of the barrel and removed the firebox water-tubes which had already become obsolete practice. During the ensuing 7 years the other 65 engines were similarly rebuilt, but from 1924 onwards the 'Maunsell' type superheater was adopted and wherever present, the 'Eastleigh' type was superseded. No 726 received in succession a superheater of each type in the course of the change-over year. The following comparison applies to a T9 of Groups (B) or (C) before and after the above alterations which, incidentally, left the overall chimney height unchanged at 13ft $2\frac{3}{4}$in.

	As built	*As rebuilt*
Heating surface (sq ft)		
Tubes (280 × $1\frac{1}{2}$)	1187	—
,, (115* × $1\frac{3}{4}$in)	—	610
,, (21 × $5\frac{1}{4}$in)	—	311
Water tubes (61 × $2\frac{3}{4}$in)	165	—
Firebox	148	142
Total Evaporative	1500	1063
Superheater	—	213
Weight in working order	48 tons 17cwt	51 tons 16cwt

* Estimated.

The superheating surface given above is the final figure; that of the original 'Eastleigh' superheater is recorded as 195sq ft. The snifting valves which accompanied the Maunsell superheater were gradually removed from their position near the top of the smokebox.

The power class was H.

From 1923 onwards the whole class was gradually provided with superheaters and extended smokeboxes, and Drummond's chimney replaced by Urie's rather more austere semi stovepipe. The Exhibition engine 773 was one of the first to be so treated, photographed at Plymouth Friary in 1924

No 714 at Plymouth in 1936, with sandboxes combined with the front splashers removed. The chimney had also by this time been modified. This was the first T9 to be withdrawn, in March 1951. Note also the snifting valves on the smokebox behind the chimney (later removed)

No 119 was specially allocated for working royal trains, and kept in particular spick and span condition. Seen here in Eastleigh Paint Shop in 1936. Note the organ pipe whistle. The use of a comparatively small engine for this duty was dictated not only by the particular reliability of the class, but also by its wide route availability

During the war years, the T9s were painted unlined black, with the exception of No 119, which, as the 'Royal' engine, was painted green and maintained as befitted its rank by Nine Elms depot, where it was stationed.

All the 66 T9s (colloquially 'Greyhounds') were in service until 1948, and they formed the Southern Region's most numerous class of 4-4-0s. They bore the brunt of increasing loads for many years, particularly on the West of England line, where they took turns on the fastest schedules until 1926.

Nos 281/2, 300/1/4/7/10-3/36, 704/26/9 were fitted with 6-wheel tenders between 1925 and 1928 and were transferred to the SECR section, where they spent many useful years on Kent Coast expresses.

Some T9s were adapted for oil burning in 1947; 133 and 280 at Eastleigh during that period

The last 15 T9s, numbered 300–5, 307, 310–4, 336–8, differed slightly in having wider splashers, thus eliminating the separate coupling rod splashers of their predecessors. No 307 in original condition in Wandsworth cutting

No 338, with water tubes removed, with an up stopping train at Weybridge in 1922

in 1925, 15 300s were fitted with sixwheeled tenders and sent to Stewart's Lane to help out on the Kent Coast line, on which they acquitted themselves right up to World War II, later reinforced by six more, some from the earlier series. No 304 passes Brixton in 1929

No 30338 in BR days, at Redhill in 1954

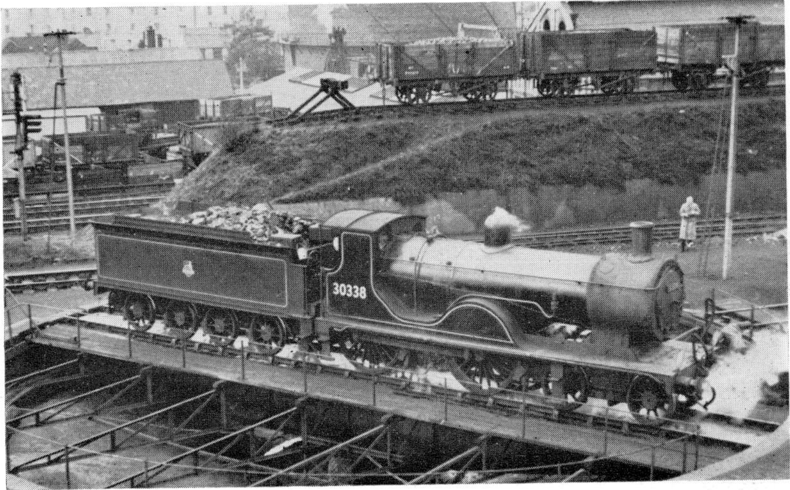

Nos 303/4/7/12 were lent to LMSR 1941 and classed for power '2P'. **No 304** was returned 28/4/45, **No 312** in Feb., 1942, and the other two in 1941. **No 304** was stationed successively at Bath and Templecombe sheds (LMSR).

No 314, was the first T9 superheated. April 1922.

No 710, was the last T9 superheated. July 1929.

No 773 renumbered **733** (previously borne by Drummond's 4–2–4 Inspection Car) in 1924 to make way for a 'King Arthur' Class engine under construction.

No 119, in 6/35, was specially painted with lined-out wheel tyres and bosses, and black shading to the tender characters, for HM King George V's journey to Portsmouth for the Jubilee Naval Review. For this duty, loose plates, with the royal arms emblazoned, were prepared for attaching to the driving splashers and the engine was fitted with a hooter. The 1935 livery lasted in splendid condition until 1946 when it was repainted in malachite green, which livery it retained even after becoming BR 30119 right to the end.

Nos 113-115, 118, 121, 280, 286, 303, 305, 314, 713, 722, and **731** were converted to oil burning in 1947/8, but on the abandonment of this short-lived phase in October 1948 they were placed aside and never ran again. All were condemned in 1951, these being amongst the first withdrawals of the class.

No	*Order No*	*Date*	*Works No*	*Rblt*	*Wdn*
113	G.9–1	6/99	565	1925	1951
114	G.9–2	,,	566	1927	1951
115	G.9–3	7/99	567	,,	1951
116	G.9–4	,,	568	1925	1951
117	G.9–5	,,	569	1927	1961
118	G.9–6	,,	570	1928	1951
119	G.9–7	8/99	571	{1923 1925	1952
120	G.9–8	,,	572	1927	1963†
121	G.9–9	9/99	573	{1924 1927	1951
122	G.9–10	,,	574	1926	1951
280	K.9–1	10/99	575	1927	1951
281	K.9–2	11/99	576	1928	1951
282	K.9–3	,,	577	{1923 1925	1954
283	K.9–4	,,	578	1925	1957
284	K.9–5	,,	579	{1923 1926	1958
285	O.9–1	1/00	580	1925	1958
286	O.9–2	2/00	581	1926	1951
287	O.9–3	,,	582	{1923 1925	1961
288	O.9–4	,,	583	1926	1960
289	O.9–5	,,	584	1927	1959
300	T.9–1	12/00	605	{1922 1925	1961
301	T.9–2	,,	606	{1923 1925	1959
302	T.9–3	,,	607	{1923 1925	1952
303	T.9–4	1/01	608	{1923 1926	1951
304	T.9–5	,,	609	{1922 1925	1957
305	X.9–1	2/01	610	{1922 1925	1951
307	X.9–2	,,	611	{1924 1925	1952
310	X.9–3	4/01	613	{1923 1925	1959
311	X.9–4	,,	614	{1922 1925	1952
312	X.9–5	5/01	615	1925	1952
313	G.10–1	,,	616	{1922 1925	1961
314	G.10–2	,,	617	{1922 1925	1951

No	*Order No*	*Date*	*Works No*	*Rblt*	*Wdn*
336	G.10–3	9/01	622	{1923 1925	1953
337	G.10–4	,,	623	1925	1958
338	G.10–5	10/01	624	{1922 1925	1961
702		1899	3746	{1923 1925	1959
703		,,	3747	1926	1952
704		,,	3748	{1923 1925	1951
705		,,	3749	{1924 1925	1958
706		,,	3750	1925	1959
707		,,	3751	1924	1961
708		,,	3752	1927	1957
709		,,	3753	{1923 1925	1961
710		,,	3754	1929	1959
711		,,	3755	1927	1959
712		,,	3756	1928	1958
713		,,	3757	1925	1951
714		,,	3758	{1924 1925	1951
715		,,	3759	{1923 1925	1961
716		,,	3760	1927	1951
717		,,	3761	,,	1961
718		,,	3762	1928	1961
719		,,	3763	1926	1961
721		,,	3764	{1923 1925	1958
722		,,	3765	{1923 1928	1951
723		,,	3766	1928	1951
724		,,	3767	{1923 1926	1959
725		,,	3768	1926	1952
726		,,	3769	{1924 1924	1959
727		,,	3770	1925	1958
728		1900	3771	1926	1956
729		,,	3772	{1923 1927	1961
730		,,	3773	1927	1957
731		,,	3774	,,	1951
732		,,	3775	,,	1959
773 733*		1901	4038	{1923 1925	1952

Nos between 113 and 338 built at Nine Elms. The others by Dübs, Glasgow.

Rblt—Rebuilt with Superheater. Where two dates are given, the first is when rebuilt with 'Eastleigh' superheater, and the second (or where only one date appears), with Maunsell superheaters.

* New number 12/24.

† No 120, restored to LSWR livery and preserved.

No 329, Class K10, in original condition, with small cross-firebox water tubes

K10 Class Mixed Traffic 4–4–0

Total in class: 40. Built: LSWR 1901–2

Like Adams before him, Drummond found that he had to provide a fleet of mixed traffic engines for the particular needs of the LSWR. His answer to this requirement lay in a 4–4–0 with 5ft 7in wheels, of which 80 were built between 1901 and 1907. They were of two Classes, K10 and L11, but, substantially the same. They earned the nickname of 'Grasshoppers', said to be owing to their great propensity for slipping, although the exact connection is not too evident. However, they performed many years of useful work on all kinds of duties, and apart from minor modifications such as the eventual removal of the firebox water tubes, were never rebuilt. The first 40, known as the K10 Class or 'Small Hoppers', had cylinders, boiler and firebox identical with those of Class C8, but the K10 boiler was pitched 7ft 6in instead of 7ft 9in, and the firebox contained 40 water tubes, 2¾in diameter, heating surface 100sq ft, by which amount the K10 total hs exceeded the C8 figure. Needless to say, the water tubes eventually disappeared; Urie began removing them quite early in his career.

The K10 frame length and wheelbase, total and divided, were identical with those of the C8s, but the K10 coupled wheels were, of course, smaller—5ft 7in diameter—and the engine weight in working order was 2cwt less—46 tons 14cwt, of which 32 tons 12cwt were on the coupled wheels. The total weights, with one or other kind of tender, are therefore the C8 figures correspondingly reduced Power class was 'F'.

The standard Drummond 6-wheel tender, 14ft wheelbase, has always been the regulation equipment for Class K10, but they allotted 7 Drummond 4,000 gallon bogie tenders which were liable to 'make the rounds', though for some years they were coupled to Nos 135/44, 380/2/6/91/2.

Withdrawal of this class began on January 4th, 1947, when four, Nos 136, 149, 342, 344 were cut up together. The K10s were always been fitted with the vacuum brake complete, and at an early date, their equipment included Drummond's patent spark arrester, which he had evolved by 1903 out of his experiments on Classes M7 and 700.

No	Order No	Date	Works No	Wdn	No	Order No	Date	Works No	Wdn
135	V.10–4	8/02	648	1949	342	K.10–5	12/01	629	1947
136	V.10–5	,,	649	1947	343	K.10–4	,,	628	1948
137	A.11–1	9/02	650	1949	344	L.10–1	,,	630	1947
138	A.11–2	,,	651	1947	345	L.10–2	1/02	631	1949
139	A.11–3	10/02	652	1948	347	L.10–3	2/02	632	1947
140	A.11–4	,,	653	1950	380	P.10–1	4/02	635	1949
141	A.11–5	,,	654	1949	381	P.10–2	,,	636	1947
142	C.11–1	11/02	655	1950	382	P.10–3	,,	637	1950
143	C.11–2	,,	656	1948	383	P.10–4	,,	638	1949
144	C.11–3	,,	657	1949	384	P.10–5	,,	639	1951
145	C.11–4	12/02	658	1948	385	S.10–1	5/02	640	1949
146	C.11–5	,,	659	1948	386	S.10–2	,,	641	1949
149	E.11–1	,,	660	1947	387	S.10–3	,,	642	1947
150	E.11–2	,,	661	1948	388	S.10–4	,,	643	1947
151	E.11–3	,,	662	1950	389	S.10–5	6/02	644	1951
152	E.11–4	,,	663	1949	390	V.10–1	,,	645	1950
153	E.11–5	,,	664	1949	391	V.10–2	7/02	646	1949
329	K.10–1	12/01	625	1950	392	V.10–3	,,	647	1948
340	K.10–2	,,	626	1948	393	L.10–4	2/02	633	1949
341	K.10–3	,,	627	1949	394	L.10–5	3/02	634	1949

Nos 135/7/8, 388/9 were lent in 1941 to LMSR for working on the Somerset and Dorset Joint line. In 8/42, **Nos 137/8** were at Gloucester, and **No 135** at Bristol. Later, these three engines were at Nottingham, whence they were returned to their owners 12/44. The other two, **Nos 388/9,** were at Bristol until their return to the SR 3/45.

No 137 was the 650th engine built at Nine Elms.

Nos 137/8, 140/1, 150, 345, 384/4, 393/4 were sent to work on the SECR section after the 1923 grouping, and on being transferred were fitted with Urie 'stovepipe' chimneys. In 11/46, **No 140** had the Drummond type chimney restored, and the smokebox wings were removed.

No 394 was lent to the War Dept. in 1941 and returned 1942.

No 30382 was the only one which survived actually to carry a BR number.

No 137, with Urie chimney and with water tubes and smokebox wingplates removed, at Exeter in 1945. This engine was one which worked on the SE&CR section early in the Grouping years

No 440, with original larger cross-firebox water tubes, running through Clapham Junction in 1920. This engine was fitted with Westinghouse brake gear

L11 Class Mixed Traffic 4–4–0

Total in class: 40. Built: LSWR 1903–7

After completing the K10 Class just described, Drummond decided to adopt the 7ft 4in firebox and the 10ft coupled wheelbase to suit, for further engines of the type. Hence the evolution of K10, which was the C8 design modified for mixed traffic, into L11 ('Large Hoppers'), which was similarly the T9 design adapted with 5ft 7in coupled wheels, and the later type of T9 boiler with 61 2¾in firebox water tubes and pitched 7ft 9in, 3in higher than the K10 centre, to allow for the 3in deeper T9 firebox.

The 10ft L11 coupled wheelbase increased the relevant K10 dimensions, already quoted, by exactly 1ft, and brought the wheelbase and overall dimensions to the T9 values, which need not be repeated. The weight of the new engine in working order was 50 tons 11cwt, of which respectively 18 tons 10cwt + 16 tons 9cwt = 34 tons 19cwt rested on the coupled wheels.

Drummond's 6-wheel outside-frame tender was standard equipment for this class. Nos 174/5, 405–13 (11 engines) were built with 4,000 gallon bogie tenders, and the many of the L11s were later so provided through tender interchange with the T9s. Five L11s, Nos 164/6, 405, 435/9, had 4,500 gallon bogie tenders of the type introduced by Drummond in 1911. These tenders were somewhat lighter (44 tons, equally distributed) than the 4,000-gallon ones, but the wheel diameter, 3ft 7in, and wheelbase (5ft 0in + 4ft 6in + 5ft 0in = 14ft 6in) are the same, and the overall length is increased by only ⅛in, which is accounted for in the tender buffers. Power class was 'F'.

Both types of bogie tender had the customary feed water heater in the tender well, and this comprised a grid of 65 tubes, 18ft 0in × 1¼in, giving 382sq ft of feed water heating surface.

The L11s were built with Drummond's patent spark arrester, and were equipped with the vacuum brake complete. Nos 440/1 also had Westinghouse brake control and retained it until some time between 1931 and 1936.

At the time when this class appeared, Drummond discarded his elliptical brass number-plate and the L11s displayed the familiar transfer numerals, which remained standard until the Grouping.

No	Order No	Date	Works No	Wdn	No	Order No	Date	Works No	Wdn	No	Order No	Date	Works No	Wdn
134	D.12–1	4/04	706	1951	168	D.12–5	5/04	710	1950	410	M.13–1	6/06	782	1949
148	D.12–2	,,	707	1952	169	F.12–1	8/04	719	1949	411	M.13–2	,,	783	1952
154	L.11–1	5/03	677	1951	170	F.12–2	,,	720	1952	412	M.13–3	7/06	783	1950
155	L.11–2	,,	678	1951	171	F.12–3	9/04	721	1951	413	M.13–4	,,	785	1951
156	L.11–3	6/03	679	1951	172	F.12–4	,,	722	1952	414	M.13–5	,,	786	1951
157	L.11–4	,,	680	1952	173	F.12–5	,,	723	1951	435	P.13–3	10/06	791	1949
158	L.11–5	,,	681	1950	174	K.13–1	5/06	775	1951	436	P.13–4	11/06	794	1951
159	O.11–1	9/03	688	1951	175	K.13–2	,,	776	1951	437	P.13–5	12/06	797	1952
161	O.11–2	,,	689	1950	405	P.13–1	9/06	788	1951	438	S.13–1	3/07	802	1951
163	O.11–3	,,	690	1951	406	P.13–2	,,	789	1951	439	S.13–2	,,	803	1949
164	O.11–4	10/03	691	1951	407	K.13–3	5/06	777	1950	440	S.13–3	4/07	804	1949
165	O.11–5	,,	692	1951	408	K.13–4	,,	778	1951	441	S.13–4	5/07	805	1951
166	D.12–3	4/04	708	1950	409	K.13–5	,,	779	1951	442	S.13–5	,,	806	1951
167	D.12–4	5/04	709	1949										

In their last years, some engines had the smokebox wing plates removed (K10 Class also).

Nos 148, 154, 155, 157, 170, 172, 411 and 437 were converted to oil burning under the 1947 scheme, but when this was abandoned in late 1948 they were laid aside as were their T9 counterparts, and like them, never ran again, although not officially withdrawn until 1951/2.

Although all 40 engines were taken into BR stock in 1948, only Nos 30134, 30156/9, 30163/4/6, 30171/3–5, 30405–7/9, 30438 and 30442, actually carried their new numbers.

No 389 with the through Plymouth – Brighton train, near Dean in 1935, and right, 439, with water tubes and smokebox wingplates removed, working a special through Eastleigh in 1939

No 170 converted for oil burning in 1948. All the class originally had six-wheeled tenders, but some of the larger 4–4–0s later exchanged their eight-wheelers for smaller tenders from the K10s and L11s

Class S11 No 395 in original condition

S11 Class Mixed Traffic 4–4–0

Total in class: 10. Built: LSWR 1903

After the L11 Class just described, Drummond produced at Nine Elms a similar design with 6ft driving wheels, Nos 395–404, which were really mixed traffic engines although intended for working express trains over the heavily graded section between Salisbury and Exeter.

In these engines, Drummond made an important technical advance in employing a built-up mild steel crank axle, in which the crank webs were extended in a direction contrary to the crank pins, so that the 'tail' thus formed acted as a counterbalance, and obviated the need for balance weights in the driving wheels. This balanced crank was a Drummond invention for which he took out patent rights, and Class S11 comprised the first British engines so balanced.

The S11 design incorporated a T9 frame, 19in × 26in cylinders, coupled wheels as above, and a boiler larger in barrel diameter, 4ft 9in, and higher pitched, 8ft 6in centre above rail, but otherwise of the same external dimensions. The heating surface was increased by a total of 50sq ft, thus: 247 1¾in tubes 1,222sq ft, 61 2¾in firebox water tubes, 165sq ft, firebox, 163sq ft, total 1,550sq ft.

The T9 working pressure, firebox length, grate area and engine wheelbase (divided and total) remained unchanged, and the tender was of the double-bogie type, the external dimensions of which were given under the C8 heading. This tender, as fitted to S11, had a tubular feed-water heater in the well, comprising 65 1¼in × 18ft tubes, with a total heating surface of 382sq ft.

Commencing with No 399 in June, 1920, by which date the firebox water tubes had been removed from the S11s as a whole, Urie fitted the 'Eastleigh' superheater to all these engines, and the heating surface was re-distributed as follows: 136 1¾in tubes, 682sq ft, 21 5¼in flues, 311sq ft, firebox 161sq ft, total evaporative hs 1,154sq ft, superheating surface 195sq ft, total combined hs 1,349sq ft. More recently, this type of superheater was superseded by the Maunsell type, which provided 213sq ft of superheating surface, the evaporative hs remaining unaltered. The working pressure was 175lb as before.

The original S11 engines weighed 52 tons in working order, distributed 17 tons 0cwt + 18 tons 0cwt + 17 tons 0cwt. The present weight is as follows. Engine, 18 tons 2cwt + 18 tons 10cwt + 17 tons 3cwt, total 53 tons 15cwt.

Tender 44 tons 17cwt, distributed as quoted under Class C8. Total (E&T), 98 tons 12cwt in working order. The total wheelbase and overall length are as follows. With bogie tender, dimensions as in Class T9, Group (C). With six-wheeled tender, as in Class T9, Group (A).

Other final developments included the removal of superheater snifters, and the replacement of the short Drummond-type chimney by the plain stove pipes of Urie design. The engines were in power Class E.

No	*Order No*	*Date*	*Works No*	*(E)*	*(M)*	*Wdn*	*No*	*Order No*	*Date*	*Works No*	*(E)*	*(M)*	*Wdn*
395	S.11–1	6/03	682	1921	1930	1951	400	V.11–1	9/03	687	1921	1931	1954
396	S.11–2	,,	683	1922	1925	1951	401	V.11–2	11/03	693	1922	1930	1951
397	S.11–3	7/03	684	1931	1931	1951	402	V.11–3	,,	694	1922	1929	1951
398	S.11–4	,,	685	1922	1930	1951	403	V.11–4	12/03	695	1921	1929	1951
399	S.11–5	8/03	686	1920	1931	1951	404	V.11–5	,,	696	1921	1931	1951

(*E*)—Date fitted with 'Eastleigh' superheater.
(*M*)—Date fitted with 'Maunsell' superheater.

These engines spent most of their time in the West Country, for which they were intended, and were rarely seen in London except for a period between 1921 and 1926 when they worked over the Portsmouth road (at one time all ten of them were stationed at Fratton).

They were all lent to the LMSR in 1941, and although they were generally shedded on the Somerset & Dorset section, they occasionally went further afield, and worked from Saltley, Burton and Peterborough. Classed for power 2P by that company, they were returned at the following dates: Nos 403–4, 30/12/44, Nos 395–6–7, 6/1/45, No 402 3/3/45, and the remaining four in April, 1945.

All except No 401 survived to carry their BR numbers 30395–30404. The last survivor, No 30400, worked from Guildford shed over the Reading-Redhill route.

Double-headed trains were something of a rarity on the LSWR, but here is 403 piloting T9 No 721, entering Devonport Tunnel in 1928

No 404, rebuilt with superheater, leaving Basingstoke with a mixed train in 1926

No 397 in Eastleigh paint shop, 1928

No 30396 in final form with Urie chimney and in BR lined black livery

Corresponding to the S11 Class were the L12s, with the customary 6in larger wheel for working on the eastern ends of the system; 20 engines, 415–434, were built 1904/5. No 419, working an express train when first built

L12 Class Express 4–4–0

Total in class: 20. Built: LSWR 1904-5

The preceding mixed-traffic Class, S11, was followed by an adaptation of the design to express work, and in June, 1904, Nine Elms turned out No 415, Class L12, an engine which differed from S11 principally in having 6ft 7in coupled wheels, and the boiler pitched 8ft 6in higher to suit.

Excepting these two dimensions, all the figures quoted for the S11s in their original form apply to Class L12, and the evolution of both classes from Class T9 is apparent when it is remembered that the T9 frame design was used throughout.

The later history of the L12s is akin to that of the S11s, but the work of superheating began at an earlier date, viz, No 421 (1915), after which the scheme was postponed until the war had ended. Reference to an illustration, which is dated 1915, shows balance weights in the driving wheels, inferring absence of the balanced cranks originally fitted, whereas the more modern picture of No 424 suggests the employment of Drummond's original balancing.

It is interesting, though not exceptional in British practice generally, that in both the S11 and L12 rebuilds, the slide valves were retained in conjunction with a fairly high degree of superheat.

The 'Eastleigh' superheater was superseded by the Maunsell type, and the data in both cases are as given under the S11 heading. The engine weight (wo) increased from 53 tons 4cwt original to 55 tons 5cwt with 'Eastleigh' or 'Maunsell' superheater, distributed 18 tons 14cwt + 19 tons 0cwt + 17 tons 11cwt, the tender weight remaining at 44 tons 17cwt throughout, wherever the bogie tender was in use.

One half of the total number of L12s retained this kind of tender, and for some years after superheating the tubular feed water heaters were maintained, and boiler feed was by means of hot water injectors.

No 428, rebuilt with superheater, leaving Wimbledon Park carriage sidings with a main line stock train for Waterloo, in April 1925

No 422, with six-wheeled tender, working on the SECR section with an up express, passing Ashford in 1925

No 424, fitted as an oilburner, at Nine Elms in 1921

No 30432 at Romsey in 1949, as finally running. This one escaped the later rather ugly Urie chimney, which most of the class eventually acquired

The other half of the total number, viz, Nos 416/7/9, 421/2/4/5, 430/1/3, for many years worked with six-wheeled tenders of 3,500 gallons capacity, and in this instance the wheelbase data and overall length dimension are as quoted for T9, Group (A).

Both classes, S11 and L12, were always fitted with vacuum brake complete, and the Urie chimney became general on most of the class. Removal of the superheater snifters, accompanied the adoption of the Maunsell superheater. Power Class was D.

No	*Order No*	*Date*	*Works No*	*(E)*	*(M)*	*Wdn*	*No*	*Order No*	*Date*	*Works No*	*(E)*	*(M)*	*Wdn*
415	L.12–1	6/04	714	1920	1927	1953	425	R.12–1	11/04	729	1920	1925	1951
416	L.12–2	,,	715	1919	1925	1951	426	R.12–2	12/04	730	1919	1926	1951
417	L.12–3	,,	716	1921	,,	1951	427	R.12–3	,,	731	1922	1925	1951
418	L.12–4	7/04	717	1919	1929	1951	428	R.12–4	1/05	732	1920	,,	1951
419	L.12–5	,,	718	,,	1925	1951	429	R.12–5	,,	733	1922	1927	1951
420	O.12–1	9/04	724	1922	1926	1951	430	T.21–1	2/05	734	1919	1925	1951
421	O.12–2	,,	725	1915	1925	1951	431	T.12–2	,,	735	1921	,,	1951
422	O.12–3	10/04	726	1920	,,	1951	432	T.12–3	,,	736	1920	,,	1951
423	O.12–4	,,	737	1919	1926	1951	433	T.12–4	3/05	737	1919	,,	1951
424	O.12–5	11/04	728	,,	1925	1951	434	T.12–5	,,	738	1922	1928	1955

(*E*)—Date fitted with 'Eastleigh' superheater.
(*M*)—Date fitted with 'Maunsell' superheater.

No 421, the first engine superheated in later years, achieved unenviable notoriety in the small hours of July 1st, 1906, when working an Up American Boat Special through Salisbury Station. Rounding the curve at excessively high speed, which has been ascribed, rightly or wrongly, to momentary drowsiness on the part of its crew, the engine came off the road and derailed the train, with a considerable loss of life. A memorial tablet to the victims of this disaster, the most serious in South Western history, may be seen in Salisbury Cathedral.

Nos 415, 423, and 424, were temporary fitted for oil burning during the 1921 coal strike, and the same thing happened in the general strike of 1926, the engines in this case being Nos 415, 420, and 424.

Ten engines, Nos 416, 417, 419, 421, 422, 424, 425, 430, 431, and 433 were transferred temporarily to the SE&CR section in 1925, being fitted with 6-wheeled tenders for the purpose, which they exchanged with 'Grasshoppers' (Class K10 and L11). They returned later to their native section, although some of them returned to the SE&CR for a time in the later 1930s.

All except No 430 survived to carry their BR numbers 30415–30434.

No 30434, which outlasted the others by several years, spent its declining days working from Guildford over the Reading-Redhill route.

The Drummond Bug in Eastleigh shed in 1922, in which position it remained for many years. The only occasion it was ever moved was when it was, very rarely (for it was usually hemmed in by about half a dozen engines on either side), found possible to have it placed outside for the benefit of photographers.

Of interest is that this view is one of the very rare pictures ever taken of the right hand side of the engine, nearly all known views being of the left hand. This may be because on the aforesaid rare occasions when it could be photographed outside, it would inevitably be on the south, or sunny side from which it was taken

F9 Class Inspection Saloon 4–2–4T

Total in class: 1. Built: LSWR 1899

For his own private use Drummond built in 1899 this little 4–2–4T combined engine and coach nicknamed 'The Bug' in which he not only 'commuted' from his home at Surbiton, but travelled all over the system. News of its approach would be greeted with a general feeling of alarm and foreboding of trouble!

After his death in 1912 it was used to some extent by the Engineering Department for inspection purposes, but from 1916 it did no work at all and lay in store in Eastleigh shed, as shown in the illustration taken in 1922. There it remained until 1932, the only thing that happened to it being in the change of its number from 733 to 58S in the service list. It still carried LSWR livery (and the pre-1918 style at that) being at that time the last engine on any of the four groups still nominally in service to carry the initials of a pre-Grouping company.

The leading dimensions were as follows. Outside cylinders, $11\frac{1}{2}$in × 18in. Wheel diameter, driving 5ft 7in, bogie 2ft 6in, those of the leading bogie spaced at 5ft, those of the trailing bogie at 8ft. The boiler barrel, 3ft 4in × 8ft 0in, pitched 6ft 6in above rail, contained 117 tubes, $1\frac{3}{4}$in diameter, heating surface 500sq ft, to which the firebox added 50sq ft, total hs 550 sq ft. Working pressure, 175lb, grate area 11·3sq ft, tank capacity 1,000 gallons, coal 1 ton. Total wheelbase 27ft $4\frac{1}{2}$in, total length over buffers 35ft $9\frac{1}{4}$in. Weight in working order, 9 tons 3cwt + 13 tons 12cwt + 14 tons 13cwt, total 37 tons 8cwt.

The coachwork comprised one compartment, lit by gas (which also supplied one lamp in the cab) with a table, an umbrella stand and a small buffet, and electric bell communication to the footplate. Through a circular window in the rear cab partition, Drummond could see what was afoot on the engine. The remaining accommodation was represented by a lavatory which occupied one of the forward corners.

Originally, the engine portion was liveried in the standard loco colours, and the saloon portion in the coaching style of its period, salmon above the waist and chocolate brown below. The running number appeared on the waist panel of the coach and not on the engine, and the panel immediately below bore the Company's coat-of-arms.

In 12/13, No 733 was relegated to the service stock, and in 12/24, the SR renumbered the unit 58S in the service vehicle list, but did not repaint the coachwork. After years of little use, the unit was brought out of storage, and in 2/32 was sent to take visiting parties round the extensive new docks then in progress at Southampton, for which purpose it was coupled to an ex-SER 6-wheel saloon, No 0824S.

No 58S reported for this duty in a fresh-looking coat of standard SR green, and still carried its own particular headcode of three diminutive *cast-iron* discs, white with a thin red border. On completing its allotted service, 58S was stored in Eastleigh paint shop, and there was some talk of preserving it, but it was not used again and finally, in 8/40 it was dismantled. The saloon later served as a hut in Eastleigh Carriage Works, and is still in existence; it is understood to be intended for conversion to a refreshment room at the premises of the Hampshire Narrow Gauge Society.

No 733, built 4/99, was the 563rd engine produced at Nine Elms. It was not classed for power, but had a good, if sometimes uncomfortable, capacity for speed. Apart from being the last 'single' on the SR, it was the last Drummond engine to retain the boiler feed clacks attached to the underhang of the smokebox tube plate. The vacuum brake was fitted to this engine, but the braking power must have been very limited, applied as it was to the driving wheels only, through the medium of only one pair of brake blocks.

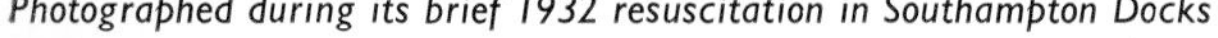

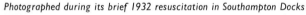

Photographed during its brief 1932 resuscitation in Southampton Docks

Drummond's first steam railcar, built in 1903 for the Fratton – Southsea branch, one of two constructed for this service.

Steam Motor-cars

Early in the twentieth century, British railways were faced with a new and formidable competitor in the shape of electric tramways, which rapidly became so widespread and popular that increasing numbers of passengers forsook the railways and took to the new and attractive form of transport for local journeys.

To stem this loss, the railways had to find a way to reduce operating expenses while increasing the frequency of local services, and Drummond led the way in finding a solution. For the short branch line from Fratton to East Southsea which was jointly owned with the LBSCR and lay in danger from an excellent tram service paralleling its entire route, he designed and put into traffic a steam railcar, comprising a small engine and a suitable coach mounted upon a single underframe carried upon a 2–2–0 front-driving motor bogie at one end and upon an ordinary four-wheeled bogie at the other.

This was Joint Steam Car No 1, the first of its kind and the forerunner of many throughout the country. The locomotive portion was a small tank engine with vertical boiler, 7in × 10in cylinders, Walschaerts valve-gear and single-driving wheels 2ft 9in diameter which was also the wheel diameter throughout. The wheels had solid disc centres, and each bogie wheelbase was 8ft. The car was designed to attain a speed of 30 mph in 30 seconds from rest, and could be driven from either end, for which purpose electric communication was provided between the footplate and the driving position at the other end of the unit. Seating accomodation totalled 42, divided into 12 first-class and 30 third-class, and the guard's compartment, adjoining the engine, had space for one ton of luggage. Two cars to this design were put in hand on Order No K11, of which the first, after experimental trips over the GWR at Stroud (Glos.) went into the East Southsea Service on June 1st, 1903, displacing the ordinary rolling stock.

It was soon found that the vertical boiler, which had both vertical fire tubes and cross-water-tubes, did not steam well, and the ordinary trains were re-instated while the motor units went back to Nine Elms for rebuilding. In October, 1903, the locomotive of No 2 car was fitted with a horizontal-type boiler, barrel 3ft 6in diameter, 1ft $2\frac{1}{8}$in long containing 155 tubes 18in long and $1\frac{1}{2}$in diameter, and 119 $1\frac{3}{4}$in firebox water tubes; the various heating surfaces are tabled below. Later the companion locomotive, No 1, was similarly rebuilt and the two units thereafter worked the East Southsea branch until the passenger service was withdrawn during the first week of World War I.

The engine portion of these cars was painted in the standard LSWR colours, and the coachwork is said originally to have been done out in the LSWR carriage livery, brown and salmon pink, but at a very early date the coachwork appeared in the then new LBSC colours, chocolate and cream. Both units were stationed at Fratton, and the terminal layout at East Southsea was simplified by means of a short diversion line to a small timber platform. The original terminal station and its extensive yard and signal box thereupon fell into disuse, and the yard has since been obliterated by streets and houses, but the original station buildings are still in existence as a garage.

After their withdrawal from the service, the two cars lay more or less derelict. No 1 was sent to Brighton, and stood for some time in the summer of 1919 behind Preston Park Paint Shop with some LBSC E4 0–6–2 tank engines lately returned from service in France. No 2 was also in existence at this period; for details, see below.

In 1904, Drummond built two more cars of a different design for working the Basingstoke & Alton Light Railway, which they took over on July 1 of that year. In these cars, the locomotive was placed back to front, so that the footplate and firebox were over the leading axle, which was also the driving axle, and the smokebox adjoined the car body. The first-class compartment was immediately next to the engine, and the guard's compartment was at the trailing end of the unit. In between was the third-class compartment, separated from the forward first-class section by an open-sided platform protected by collapsible trellis gates.

These cars were originally Nos 1 and 2 in the LSWR stock list, but they were afterwards allotted the carriage list numbers, 4201, 4202. In summer time, one of them was regularly transferred to Plymouth Friary, to work the Turnchapel branch.

This design was finally developed into Nos 3 to 15 inclusive, after which no more were built. A major disadvantage had become apparent, namely, that

The vertical boiler was found to be too small, and the railcars later received horizontal boilers as shown. They were the joint property of the LSWR and the LB&SCR as Joint stock Nos 1 and 2

LSWR steam railcar No 2, with enclosed engine

A still later design, No 5, with the engine covering designed to match the coach body

minor repairs, which the engine portion so often needed, meant either laying aside the entire unit or else using an ordinary engine to haul it 'dead', as was done on the East Southsea line.

Cars Nos 3 to 15 were unlike their companions inasmuch as the entire unit was encased in coachwork and uniformly painted in the carriage livery. The engine portion was again placed back to front, but immediately next to it came the third-class compartment and at the trailing end were grouped together the first-class compartment, luggage and guard's compartment and driver's control cab. These cars, Nos 3–15, were afterwards numbered 4203–4215 in the carriage list.

The first World War made the steam cars redundant, since it was not policy to encourage additional traffic, and all of the LSWR cars, except Nos 4203, 4204 and 4210 were withdrawn from stock in October, 1916. The survivors lasted until July, 1919, but it was reported in 1920 that No 10 had been converted to a trailer car for the ordinary pull-and-push service. The joint car, No 2, was reported converted at the same time.

The cars built to Order H13 were for local use in the following areas: Bournemouth, Bodmin and Wadebridge, Friary and Turnchapel, Whitchurch and Fullerton. The similar cars Nos 12 and 13, Order A14 were used between Exeter and Topsham, and the last two worked between Bentley and Bordon Camp. In September, 1912, Nos 12 and 14 were at Strawberry Hill for the Twickenham local routes, in June, 1913, Nos 1, 2 and 11 were in Eastleigh depot and No 4 in the Works yard, and in April, 1915, No 13 was at Strawberry Hill depot.

All the Drummond steam cars were fitted with the vacuum brake, and were lit by gas. The engine portion and the frame were built at Nine Elms, and sent down to Eastleigh Carriage Works, where the bodies were built and fitted. The following tables record all the principal and available data:

Car Nos	*Joint 1, 2*	*LSW 1, 2*	*LSW 3–15*
Cylinders (*in*)	7 × 10 $7\frac{3}{4}$* × 10	9 × 14	10 × 14
Wheel diameter	2′ 9″	3′ 0″	←
Working pressure (*lb psi*)	150	←	175
Boiler Pitch	NR	9′ 2″	←
Heating surface (*sq ft*):			
Tubes	94	152	←
Water tubes	119	119	←
Firebox	76	76	←
Total	289	347	←
Grate area (*sq ft*)	$6\frac{3}{4}$	←	←
Wheelbase:			
Bogie	8′ 0″	←	←
Total	47′ 11″	41′ 1″	42′ 4″
Weight:			
On Engine Bogie	16 tons 1cwt	22 tons $4\frac{1}{2}$cwt	21 tons 14cwt
On Car Bogie	9 tons $5\frac{1}{4}$cwt	9 tons $6\frac{1}{4}$cwt	10 tons 12cwt
Total	25 tons $6\frac{1}{4}$cwt	31 tons $10\frac{3}{4}$cwt	32 tons 6cwt
Over Buffers	56′ 4″	51′ $2\frac{1}{2}$″	52′ $6\frac{3}{4}$″
Over Chimney	11′ $11\frac{1}{2}$″	12′ 6″	13′ $0\frac{5}{8}$″
Tank Capacity (*galls*)	170	530	485
Seats:			
1st class	12	8	←
3rd class	30	32	←
Total	42	40	←

The arrow ← repeats the dimension to which it points.
NR—No record.
* After rebuilding with horizontal boiler.

The cars were divided into compartments of the following lengths, in the following sequence from the engine. Where frame lengths are given, the dimension does not include the buffers.

K11. Engine compartment, length not recorded. Luggage and Guard, 5′ 0″. Gate, 2′ 0″. Third class, 22′ $0\frac{1}{2}$″. First class, 11′ $2\frac{1}{2}$″. End gate and driver's balcony, 3′ $11\frac{1}{2}$″. Total frame 53′ 4″. After re-boilering, the smokebox overhung the buffer-beam. Boiler pitch not recorded. Over chimney 11′ $11\frac{1}{2}$″.

H12. Engine, 11′ 1″. First class, 6′ $5\frac{1}{2}$″. Third class, 21′ 10″. Luggage and Guard, 5′ $10\frac{1}{2}$″. Total body, 48′ $2\frac{1}{2}$″. Boiler pitch 9′ 2″. Over chimney 12′ 6″.

H13, A14, B14. Engine compartment encased in two lengths of coachwork, with footplate access gate between, thus: 1′ $1\frac{1}{2}$″ + 2′ 0″ (gate) + 8′ $2\frac{7}{8}$″. Third class, 21′ $9\frac{1}{4}$″. Gate, 2′ $11\frac{1}{2}$″. First class, 7′ $7\frac{3}{4}$″. Luggage and Guard, 6′ $3\frac{1}{8}$″. Total frame, 49′ $6\frac{3}{4}$″, plus $5\frac{1}{4}$″ gained by slight outward curvature of body at each end, giving 50′ 0″ total over body. Boiler pitch 9′ 2″. Over chimney 13′ $0\frac{5}{8}$″.

No	*Order No*	*Date*	*Works No*	*No*	*Order No*	*Date*	*Works No*	*No*	*Order No*	*Date*	*Works No*
Jt.1	K.11–1	5/03	675	4	H.13–2	11/05	750	10	H.13–8	12/05	760
Jt.2	K.11–2	,,	676	5	H.13–3	,,	752	11	H.13–9	1/06	762
1	H.12–1	5/04	711	6	H.13–4	,,	753	12	A.14–1	5/06	773
2	H.12–2	,,	712	7	H.13–5	12/05	754	13	A.14–2	,,	774
3	H.13–1	11/05	749	8	H.13–6	,,	756	14	B.14–1	6/06	780
				9	H.13–7	,,	758	15	B.14–2	,,	781

Motor train engine No 737, a completely independent locomotive with separate trailers

Motor-train Tank Engines

Built: LSWR

The major disadvantage of the unit-frame type motor-car, viz, that minor engine repairs immobilised the entire unit, inspired a new type, since known as 'pull and push', or 'P&P', in which a small tank engine is coupled to one or more trailer coaches provided with means whereby the engine can be controlled from the remote end of the train so made up.

For trains of this sort, which originated with Marsh's 1905 unit on the LBSCR, Drummond produced, in the following year, the first of a class of small four-wheeled tank engines, with single driving wheels, Class C14, colloquially known as the 'Potato Cans', of which ten were built at Nine Elms.

Class C14, 1906-7, Nos. 736-745 (10) 2-2-0T

The leading dimensions of these little engines, which were obviously developed from the engines of the steam-cars and had a similar arrangement of the Walschaerts valve-gear, were as follows:

Outside cylinders, situated between fore and aft pairs of wheels, 10in × 14in. Wheel diameter, leading and driving, 3ft 0in, wheelbase, 8ft 0in. The boiler, pitched 7ft 3in centre above rail, and pressed at 150lb, had a single-plate barrel, 4ft 0in external diameter × 4ft 2in long containing 216 1½in tubes giving 379sq ft of heating surface, to which 99 1¾in transverse water tubes in the firebox added 119sq ft and the firebox proper added 73sq ft, total hs 572sq ft. The firebox was 4ft 4in long outside, and the grate area 9·55sq ft.

The front overhang was 5ft 10in, rear overhang 5ft 9in, length over buffers 19ft 7in, height over chimney top, 12ft 4in. The tanks held 500 gallons of water, and the coal bunker had a capacity of 1 ton. The weight in working order was 25 tons 15cwt, of which 12 tons 11cwt were borne by the single pair of driving wheels.

Though found deficient in adhesion, owing to the non-coupled driving wheels, these engines worked various motor-train services for seven to eight years until the outbreak of war in 1914, by which date two had already been converted to coupled engines, 0–4–0T. During the war, six were sold to the Government, and these engines ultimately came under the control of the Disposals Board, which advertised them to prospective buyers for a very long time, describing them as 'A New Type', and heading the advertisements with a table of dimensions and a line drawing showing the engine lettered and lined according to LSWR

All except Nos 741, 744 and 745 were sold to the Government during World War I, but these three had many years of service not only on the SR, but lasting into BR days. No 0741 is seen here lying disused at Strawberry Hill in 1921, but like the other two was rebuilt as a 0–4–0T for use on Southampton Quayside, as shown below

A very similar scene thirty five years later. No 30589 (old 744) at almost the same location in 1957. Note taller chimney

Class S14 0–4–0T No 101

standards. One of the engines was still unsold as late as the Spring of 1922.

The first C14 converted to 0–4–0T was No 745, followed at intervals by Nos 743, 741 and 744 as shown in the table. Nos 741, 744 and 745 were still at work until the late 1950s a familiar sight along the Southampton waterfront.

Class S14, 1910, Nos. 101 and 147, 0-4-0T

These were engines distinctly resembling the C14s, but immediately distinguishable both by reason of their coupled wheels, and the position of their outside cylinders. When the original C14s were converted to coupled engines, the cylinders were similarly placed under the smokebox, and the resemblance between the two classes was correspondingly enhanced.

The S14s were, however, larger engines, with 3ft 8in wheels, 12in × 18in cylinders, 175lb working pressure, and 4 tons more of total weight.

Their history on the LSWR was brief, but they are historically important as the first two engines built at the then new Eastleigh locomotive works.

The summary of both the above classes, both of which were not classed for power, is as follows:

No	*Order No*	*Date*	*Works No*	*No*	*Order No*	*Date*	*Works No*
	Class C14				Class C14		
736	C.14–1	9/06	787	741	D.14–1	11/06	796
737	C.14–2	,,	790	742	D.14–2	12/06	798
738	C.14–3	10/06	792	743	D.14–3	,,	799
739	C.14–4	,,	793	744	D.14–4	1/07	800
740	C.14–5	11/06	795	745	D.14–5	,,	801
	Class S14				Class S14		
101	S.14–1	9/10	**1***	147	S.14–2	9/10	**2***

*Eastleigh.

DISPOSAL

736 Sold to Ministry of Munitions (Leeds), 3/17.
737 Sold to War Department (Grangemouth), 11/17.
738 Sold to Ministry of Munitions (Bridgwater), 3/17.
739 Cylinders enlarged to 11 × 14in. Sold to Bute Works Supply Co, Cardiff, 2/17, re-sold the following month to Alban Richards & Co, Bramley.
740 Sold to War Department, 12/16. Said to have been allocated to Shoeburyness Garrison Railway.
741 Cylinders enlarged to 11 × 14in. Lent to Ministry of Munitions, 4/17, Duplicated 9/19, returned to LSWR 1920. Converted to 0–4–0T, 2/22, cylinders 14 × 14in. Renumbered 3741 by SR. Became BR 30588. Withdrawn 1957.
742 Sold to Ministry of Munitions (Shoeburyness), 2/17. Worked on Shoeburyness Garrison Railway, and was still there late 1919.
743 Converted to 0–4–0T, cylinders 14 × 14in, 6/13. Sold to Admiralty (Portsmouth Dockyard), 12/17.
744 Renumbered 0744 (1918). Converted to 0–4–0T, cylinders 14 × 14in, 10/23. Renumbered 3744 by SR. Interesting as the 800th engine built at Nine Elms Works. Became BR 30589. Withdrawn 1957.
745 Converted to 0–4–0T, cylinders 10in × 14in, 3/13. Renumbered 0745 (1918). Transferred 10/27 to Engineer's Dept., Redbridge (Sleeper Depot) as No 77S. Withdrawn 1959.
101 Sold to Ministry of Munitions (Trumpington), 5/17.
147 Sold to Ministry of Munitions, 5/17.

NOTE.—After disposal of the S14 engines, Nos 101, 147, these numbers remained vacant until 1922, when the two K14 tanks, *Dinan* and *Dinard* were renumbered thus. **Nos 101** and **147** were the first engines to be built at Eastleigh Works.

No 330, the first of Drummond's five ill fated 4–6–0s Nos 330–334, Class F13, turned out in 1905. They proved very sluggish and unreliable, and were relegated to freight trains. Being intended in any case for the Salisbury – Exeter road, they were hardly ever seen in the London area, and photographs of them in action in their original condition are rare. In this view, taken at Eastleigh coal stage in 1920, the engine was in steam, and had presumably been working a train

F13, E14, E3, G14, P14 and T14 Classes Express 4–6–0

Built by L.S.W.R.

Until 1905, Drummond had built nothing larger than an eight-wheels engine for express passenger working, using, as we have seen, 6ft 7in driving wheels for the London-Salisbury section, and 6ft driving wheels for the services West of Salisbury. In the meantime, the West of England trains were marshalling an increasing proportion of heavier corridor stock, which was also steam-heated throughout, and to meet these additional demands on boiler power, Drummond introduced, in 1905, the first of an assorted range of 4-cylinder 4–6–0 engines, and none of them was conspicuously brilliant in performance. The power class was B (but see Class T14).

Class F13, 1905, Nos. 330-4 (5)

This class comprised a large engine with 6ft driving wheels, of which the intermediate pair were driven from outside cylinders with Walschaerts valve gear, and the leading pair from inside cylinders with Stephenson valve gear.

The engines were fitted with Drummond's patent spark arrester and, apart from being the largest engines in the South of England, they had the greatest total heating surface of any British locomotives.

Their life in this original form was comparatively short, for, in 1924, Maunsell renewed them into the H15 Class, by which is meant that the original engines were dismantled and certain usable parts were incorporated in the new construction. In these circumstances they are best considered a rebuilds, although some authorities prefer to classify them as completely new engines.

No 333 of this class had been experimentally rebuilt by Urie in 1920, with 'Eastleigh' superheater, extended smokebox and 'stovepipe' chimney, but very

No 333 was rebuilt with superheater in 1920, resulting in an extremely ugly engine, and without any noticeable improvement in performance. Seen at Exmouth Junction in 1924

little work was had from the engine in this condition, and it was renewed with the rest of the class.

Class E14, 1907, No. 335 (1) Rebuilt as H15, November, 1914

The 330 Class did not meet requirements and, in December, 1907, Drummond built a similar engine with cylinders increased in dimensions to $16\frac{1}{2} \times 26$in. Apparently this engine, Class E14, was less successful still, and Drummond's successor renewed it as a 2-cylinder H15 Class after less than seven years' service.

Another somewhat similar engine to the F13s was the solitary E14, No 335, which appeared in 1907. No improvement on its predecessors, it had an even shorter life, being rebuilt in 1914 by Urie as Class H15 to conform with his new engines

In 1908, Drummond tried again with five 4–6–0s class G14, Nos 453–457, and another five very similar engines, 448–452, in 1910/1. A slight improvement on the earlier machines, with much in common, they still suffered from similar faults. No 452 leaves Waterloo around 1909

The bogie tender of this engine was fitted with a water pick-up scoop, which was never used because the only suitable location for water troughs on the main line involved too much expense for their installation.

Classes E3, G14, P14, 1908-11, Nos. 448-57 (10)

This was Drummond's third 4–6–0 design, of which the first five engines, built at Nine Elms, proved sufficiently useful to warrant a further five, and these were the first tender engines turned out by the then newly-established Eastleigh locomotive works.

With one exception, no attempt was made to rebuild these engines. They were withdrawn en bloc in 1925 and this view shows Nos 455 and 453 in Eastleigh yard awaiting cutting up

The design incorporated smaller cylinders, piston valves and an appreciably smaller boiler. The bogie tenders, of which those allotted to Nos 453–7 had water scoops, held 4,500 gallons, but the wheelbase remained as before. The tenders were ultimately given to the new Maunsell 1925 'King Arthur' engines which took the G14 numbers. In this case, unlike the 330 Class, there was no question of a rebuild, as the old engine was still to be seen intact (apart from the tenders) in Eastleigh yard after the appearance of the new ones.

The above two classes, E14 and G14, externally differed from the original F13s by having a continuous wide splasher over the leading and intermediate coupled wheels. This splasher was pierced by two circular, glass-fronted inspection doors giving access to the outside valve gear. The glass was afterwards replaced by sheet metal.

Although several good runs stand to the credit of these engines, they were required to take loads of 350 tons up Honiton bank *en route* to Exeter, and at this work their anticipated success was not realised. As the South Western was competing for this traffic with the GWR, something with greater freedom in running was necessary, and this led Drummond to his final 4–6–0 design, in which the driving wheel diameter was increased to 6ft 7in.

The exception referred to was 449, which was rebuilt by Urie in 1922, with superheater and other modifications. In 1924, Maunsell, the CME after the Grouping, used it for experiments with 135deg cranks (giving eight exhausts per revolution instead of the usual four) in anticipation of his forthcoming Lord Nelson Class. In this form the engine ran until 1925. As the new King Arthur No 449 had appeared in the meantime it was placed on the duplicate list as E0449. Photographed at Salisbury, October, 1925

All the F13s were taken out of service in 1924 and entirely rebuilt as two-cylinder engines by Maunsell.
Here is No 330 with a West of England express in August, 1928

Class T14: 1911-12, Nos. 443-47, 458-62 (10)

The 6ft 7in engines just alluded to were introduced in 1911 and, among other alterations, Drummond relegated the outside cylinders to a position further forward, where they were in line with the inside cylinders. The continuous splasher was pierced by a single inspection door, and was of such large dimensions that the engines were nicknamed 'Paddleboxes'. This class was intended to work between London and Bournemouth, as well as to Salisbury.

Nos 447 and 458–62 were fitted with Drummond's smokebox superheater or 'Steam Drier', which raised the total temperature to 400 deg. This was regarded as sufficient and, moreover, it obviated serious problems of lubrication. The steam drier comprised grids of 2in diameter tubes in communication with the boiler tubes and, therefore, exposed to the hot gases of combustion. These superheating tubes were contained in chambers through which live steam was passed on its way to the steam chests.

The other four engines used saturated steam, and the entire class was fitted with the standard Drummond firebox tubes, which Urie removed as soon as occasion offered. Urie's principal contribution towards improving the T14 Class, which suffered largely from insufficient bearing surfaces in the coupled wheel journals, was to fit 'Eastleigh' superheaters of an orthodox kind, with extended smokeboxes to suit, and Maunsell also took the engines in hand, fitting superheaters of his own design, and introducing forced lubrication for the coupled wheel bearings. The Maunsell alterations improved the appearance with a new layout of the running plate which superseded the 'Paddlebox' splashers.

With the exception of No 458, which had to be cut up following a direct hit in Nine Elms shed during the war, they all lasted into BR days although only Nos 30446, 30447 and 30461 actually carried their new numbers. They latterly acquired Urie stovepipe chimneys. The tenders largest bogie type, holding 5,800 gallons of water and 5 tons of coal and originally intended for his contemporary D15 4–4–0s. The wheelbase is 16ft 6in (5ft 6in + 5ft 6in + 5ft 6in), and the weight, full, 60 tons 8cwt, distributed 30 tons 12cwt + 29 tons 16cwt, respectively on the forward and rear bogies.

As the dimensional table shows, the original T14s had the 'extra capacity' 4,500-gallon tender, but the 5,800-gallon tenders were allocated to this class at an early date, beginning with No 462 in 1912.

The T14s were in power Class 'B' till 1930/1, and 'A' subsequently.

Features common to all the Drummond 4–6–0s when new were the fire-box water tubes, and the tubular feed-water heater in the tender. The following is a complete comparison of the leading dimensions:

Drummond's final essay in the 4–6–0 field was class T14.

One big improvement was the placing of the cylinders forward, in line with the smokebox. The valves were housed behind a large casing.

No 444 in original condition working a Bournemouth express

The T14s were rebuilt with superheaters and the water tubes removed. Here at Eastleigh in 1930, No 458 was to be destroyed at Nine Elms in 1940 during an air raid

Class	*F13, E14**	*F13, No 333 Rbt 1920*	*G14*	*P14*	*T14 Original*	*T14 Rebuilt*
Cylinders (4), (*in*)	16 × 24 16½ × 26*	16 × 24	15 × 26	←	←	←
Wheel diameter:						
Bogie	3′ 7″	←	←	←	←	←
Driving	6′ 0″	←	←	←	6′ 7″	←
Boiler:						
Barrel Diameter	5′ 6″	←	4′ 10¾″	←	←	←
,, Length	13′ 9″	←	←	←	←	←
Wkg Press (*lb psi*)	175	←	←	←	200	175
Pitch above rail	9′ 0″	←	←	←	9′ 3½″	←
Firebox, length outside	9′ 6″	←	←	←	←	←
Tubes, 1¾″ how many	340	—	247	←	←	—
2″ ,, ,, ...	—	167	—	—	—	116
†2¾″ ,, ,, ...	112	—	84	←	←	—
‡5¼″ ,, ,, ...	—	24	—	—	—	21
Heating surface (*sq ft*):						
1¾″ tubes	2,210	—	1,580	←	←	—
2″ ,, ...	—	1,250	—	—	—	873
†2¾″ ,, ...	357	—	200	←	←	—
‡5¼″ ,, ...	—	464	—	—	—	407
Firebox	160	168	140	←	←	158
Superheater	—	308	—	—		§269
Total	2,727	2,192	1,920	←	←	§1,707
Grate Area (*sq ft*)	31·5	←	←	←	←	←
Wheelbase:						
Bogie	6′ 6″	←	←	←	←	←
Coupled	13′ 4″	←	←	14′ 4″	14′ 4″	←
Total (*Engine*)	26′ 5″	←	26′ 11″	26′ 11″	27′ 7″	←
Weight (*full*):						
On Coupled Wheels	56t 1c	52t 16c	50t 13c	53t 15c	52t 0c	54t 15c
Engine only	76t 13c	73t 18c	70t 19c	74t 13c	74t 10c	76t 10c
Tender	44t 17c	←	49t 0c	←	←	‖60t 8c
Engine and Tender	121t 10c	118t 15c	119t 19c	123t 13c	123t 10c	136t 18c

The arrow ← repeats the dimension to which it points.

* No 335 only, which differed from F13 only in cylinder dimensions, with some corresponding variation in engine weight.

† Firebox water tubes.

‡ Superheater flues.

§ With 'Eastleigh' superheater. With 'Maunsell' superheater, these figures are, respectively, 295sq ft, and 1,733sq ft.

‖ 5,800-gallon tender, replacing original 4,500-gallon tender.

The coupled wheelbase is, in all cases, equally divided. The bogie centre pin was, in all cases, placed 1in forward of the true bogie centre.

Boiler barrel dimensions are minimum external diameter × length from tube-plate to throat plate.

No	*Order No*	*Date*	*Works No*	*Rebuilt as H15*	*Wdn*
		F13			
330	F.13–1	4/06	768	11/24	1957
331	F.13–2	,,	679	11/24	1961
332	F.13–3	,,	770	12/24	1956
333	F.13–4	,,	771	12/24	1958
334	F.13–5	,,	772	1/25	1958
		E14			
335	E.14	12/07	807	12/14	1959
		G14			
453	G.14–1	3/08	808		1925
454	G.14–2	4/08	810		1925
455	G.14–3	,,	812		1925
456	G.14–4	5/08	813		1925
457	G.14–5	,,	814		1925

No	*Order No*	*Date*	*Works No*	*(E)*	*(M)*	*Wdn*
		F14				
448	P.14–1	10/10	**3**	—	—	1925
449	P.14–2	11/10	**4**	—	—	1927
450	P.14–3	12/10	**5**	—	—	1925
451	P.14–4	1/11	**6**	—	—	1925
452	P.14–5	2/11	**7**	—	—	1925
		T14				
443	T.14–1	3/11	**8**	1915	1931	1949
444	T.14–2	4/11	**9**	1917	,,	1950
445	T.14–3	5/11	**10**	1915	,,	1948
446	T.14–4	6/11	**11**	,,	,,	1951
447	T.14–5	,,	**12**	1917	1930	1949
458	B.15–1	12/11	**23**	1915	,,	1940
459	B.15–5	6/12	**29**	1917	1931	1948
460	B.15–2	1/12	**24**	1916	1930	1948
461	B.15–3	3/12	**26**	1918	1931	1951
462	B.15–4	4/12	**27**	1917	1930	1950

Works Nos 3 onwards were built at Eastleigh.

(*E*)—Date fitted with 'Eastleigh' superheater.

(*M*)—Date fitted with 'Maunsell' superheater.

ENGINE SUMMARY

No 449, renumbered **0449** in 1925, was the last of the 6ft engines, and prior to scrapping was converted to 135 deg. crank phase giving 8 beats for trial before adoption in the forthcoming SR 'Lord Nelson' 4–6–0s.

The huge splashers were later removed and the footplate raised to give better access, but they still remained rather ungainly engines, especially seen from the front end; they were possibly better viewed from the rear. This picture also depicts very clearly the massive 'water cart' tenders designed by Drummond, necessitated by the absence of water troughs. Clapham Junction, 1930

No 459 was originally allotted **No 463** (hence the irregular sequence in Works Nos), because the number **459** was already occupied by Drummond 700 Class 0–6–0 ex-**716**. As already noted, the 0–6–0 was renumbered **316,** and thus the numbers of the 4–6–0 engines were kept together.

Three T14s survived to be renumbered by British Railways. No 30461 in its final form, with modified chimney, at Nine Elms in 1949

No 470, in its short-lived original condition

D15 Class Express 4–4–0

Total in class: 10. Built: LSWR (Eastleigh) 1912–3

These fine 4–4–0 engines with smokebox superheater, double-bogie tenders, feed-water heating apparatus, and the usual water-tube firebox, were Drummond's last design, and he died before the entire class was completed. Improving on his 415 Class of 1904, Drummond, in the D15s, produced engines that ranked among his most successful efforts. They worked the London end of the main line, and at one time practically monopolised the Portsmouth expresses, which they continued to work until displaced by Maunsell's Schools Class.

The principal dimensions of this masterly design were as follows. Cylinders, 19½in × 26in. Wheel diameter, bogie (engine and tender), 3ft 7in, coupled 6ft 7in. Wheelbase, 6ft 6in + 8ft 3in + 10ft 0in, total (engine) 24ft 9in total (E&T) 49ft 7in, length over buffers (E&T) 59ft 2¼in.

The boiler, pressed at 200lb, and pitched 8ft 9in centre above rail, had a barrel 4ft 9½in minimum internal diameter, by 12ft 0in long (tube plate to throat plate), containing 247 1¾in diameter tubes, giving a heating surface of 1,406sq ft, to which 66 2¾in firebox water tubes added 170sq ft, and the firebox proper added 148sq ft, total hs 1,724sq ft. The firebox was 8ft 4in long outside, grate area 27sq ft. Power class was D.

The double-bogie tender, with inside bogie frames, was of the intermediate type, capacities 4,500 gallons of water, and 4 tons of coal, and in the well was the customary tubular condenser, comprising 65 1¼in tubes, giving 382sq ft of feed-water heating surface.

No 463, the first engine of this Class, was turned out with a hooter instead of a whistle, and this was on the engine for many years. The regular arrival of No 463 at Portsmouth was thus distinctively announced above the usual terminal overtones, and it remained for years a characteristic of the 'local colour'. The hooter was removed, it is said, to avoid clashing with the ARP sirens.

During World War I, Urie took all the ten D15 engines in hand, and rebuilt them with 'Eastleigh' superheater and extended smokebox, at the same time removing the firebox water-tubes, and increasing the size of the diameter of the cylinders to 20in. The pressure was reduced to 180lb, and the heating surface was modified as follows 156 1¾in tubes, 782·5sq ft, 21 5¼in tubes, 357sq ft, firebox 144·5sq ft, total evaporative hs 1,284sq ft. The superheating surface was 231sq ft, and is now 252sq ft, obtained in the 21 1⅜in elements of the 'Maunsell' superheater which has completely ousted the 'Eastleigh' type.

The fitting of 'Maunsell' superheaters more or less coincided with a replacement of tenders, whereby the D15s received those of the Drummond six-wheel outside-frame type, holding 3,500 gallons. The following comparison of maximum weights assumes a bogie tender under the heading 'Original', and a six-wheel tender under the heading 'Rebuilt'.

	Original	*Rebuilt*
On Bogie	20 tons 15cwt	21 tons 13cwt
On Driving wheels	19 tons 10cwt	20 tons 0cwt
On Trailing Coupled wheels ...	19 tons 10cwt	19 tons 18cwt
Engine total	59 tons 15cwt	61 tons 11cwt
Tender...	49 tons 0cwt	40 tons 14cwt
Total (E&T)	108 tons 15cwt	102 tons 5cwt

No 463 at the old Southampton Central station in 1922, having been rebuilt with superheater, extended smokebox, and the firebox water tubes removed. All 10 engines were stationed at Bournemouth then for the main trains to Waterloo, supplemented by an eleventh engine of the ever-versatile Class T9, No 313. No 463 was unique in having a Caledonian-type hooter in place of the normal whistle. Drummond had of course served with the CR, snd it is possible that he was considering introducing it to the South Western

No 471 with an up Bournemouth express passing Woking in 1921

All ten were fitted in 1925/6 with six-wheeled tenders (exchanged with Classes K10 and L11) for working the Portsmouth line, to enable them to get on to the turntable in Fratton roundhouse shed. No 472 at Eastleigh in 1927

No	*Order No*	*Date*	*Works No*	*(E)*	*(M)*	*Wdn*	*No*	*Order No*	*Date*	*Works No*	*(E)*	*(M)*	*Wdn*
463	D.15–1	2/12	**25**	1916	1926	1951	468	G.15–1	9/12	**33**	1916	1926	1952
464	D.15–2	5/12	**28**	1915	,,	1954	469	G.15–2	10/12	**34**	,,	1925	1951
465	D.15–3	6/12	**30**	,,	,,	1956	470	G.15–3	11/12	**35**	1917	,,	1952
466	D.15–4	7/12	**31**	1916	,,	1952	471	G.15–4	,,	**36**	,,	1926	1954
467	D.15–5	,,	**32**	1917	1925	1955	472	G.15–5	12/12	**37**	1916	,,	1952

(*E*)—Date fitted with 'Eastleigh' superheater.
(*M*)—Date fitted with 'Maunsell' superheater.
No 472 was taken into stock 1/13.

During 1925/6 all ten engines received 6-wheeled tenders by exchange with Classes K10 and L11, this was so that they could use the turntable in Fratton roundhouse shed, to which depot they were being transferred to work the Portsmouth expresses.

A new boiler for the class was built in 1925 which differed from the others in having the safety valves on the firebox instead of the normal Drummond position on the dome. This boiler appeared at various times on different members of the class. In later years all of them were somewhat disfigured by being fitted with Urie stovepipe chimneys. Nos 470 ran temporarily as an oil burner in 1921, and again in 1926, whilst No 463 was similarly adapted under the short-lived 1948 scheme. Like the other engines of Classes T9 and L11 involved, it was never re-converted, and did no further work, being scrapped in 1951 without receiving its new number. The other duly became Nos 30464–30472.

No 467 seen here with an up stopping Portsmouth train, at Liphook in 1936

No 30470 in BR days, at Southampton in 1950

CHAPTER SIX

THE URIE ENGINES

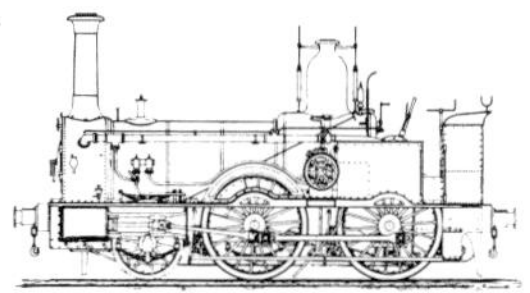

H15 Class Mixed Traffic 4–6–0

Total in class: 26. Built: LSWR (Eastleigh), S.R. 1913–25

URIE'S first design, following his accession to the post of Chief Mechanical Engineer rendered vacant by Drummond's death in 1912, was a good-looking mixed traffic 4–6–0 radically different in appearance from the Drummond engines of the type, yet claiming a certain kinship in virtue of a typical Drummond cab.

This was Class H15, of which ten engines, Nos 482–491 were built during 1913–14. In many respects, they broke with tradition, and features like Drummond's steam-drier, firebox water tubes, and inside-framed tender bogies were discarded. In so far as they were two-cylinder engines, with the cylinders outside, the H15s reverted to the policy inaugurated by the elder Beattie, and perpetuated by Adams, and from the H15s down to the end of the LSWR no more inside-cylinder engines were built. The H15 cylinders had overhead inside-admission piston valves, actuated by Walschaerts valve-gear, and the engines were distinctive with a high running-plate, which gave easy access to the motion. This was eventually, although many years later, destined to set the ultimate trend in fashion of steam locomotive design in this country.

The tender also was a novelty with its external bogie frames and large capacities, respectively 5,200 gallons of water and no less than 7 tons of coal. The wheel diameter was 3ft 7in as before, but the bogie wheelbase was increased to 6ft 6in, and total tender wheelbase to 19ft.

These engines were at first painted in the passenger livery, and it will be noted that they were the first on the LSWR with fire-tube superheaters of the normal kind. It was a rather belated adoption of the principle, but Urie wished to test for himself the merits of superheating, and therefore Nos 482–5 were fitted with Schmidt apparatus, 486–9 with Robinson's, and 490–1 were built to use saturated steam. The final result was the adoption of a superheater designed by Urie—the 'Eastleigh' type—which was subsequently fitted to Nos 490/1. The table overleaf is a comparison of heating surfaces relevant to the above superheaters and valid at date 1924.

With the above exceptions, the ten engines were identical and the following dimensions apply to all of this first lot.

Outside cylinders 21in × 28in. Wheel diameter, bogie 3ft 7in, coupled 6ft 0in. Engine wheelbase, 7ft 6in + 5ft 4½in + 6ft 3in + 7ft 6in, total 26ft 7½in.

		Saturated Steam No 490	*Schmidt Superheater Nos 482–5*	*Robinson Superheater Nos 486–9*	*'Eastleigh' Superheater Nos 490/1*
Small Tubes ...	*sq ft*	2,025	1,252	1,252	1,252
Large Tubes ...	,,	—	507	464	464
Firebox	,,	167	167	167	167
Total	,,	2,191	1,296	1,883	1,883
Superheater ...	,,	—	360	333	308
Total Combined	,,	—	2,286	2,216	2,191
Grate Area ...	,,	30	30	30	30

Boiler pitch 9ft 0in, working pressure 180lb per sq in. Barrel, 5ft 6in minimum external diameter, 13ft 9in long from tube plate to throat plate. Firebox 9ft 0in long outside. Over buffers, 65ft 6¾in. Weight (engine) in working order, 20 tons 16cwt + 20 tons 2cwt + 20 tons 4cwt + 20 tons 3cwt, total 81 tons 5cwt.

In June, 1927, Maunsell fitted No 491 with a King Arthur Class boiler pressed at 200lb, and equipped with a 'Maunsell' superheater, and subsequently 'Maunsell' superheaters were fitted to the other nine engines, but in these the original type boiler was retained.

The relevant data are as follows:

No 487 of Urie's first design, as originally built. Its somewhat unorthodox appearance at the time, with the high running plate almost clear of the driving wheels, and almost total absence of splashers, was destined eventually to set the pattern for future design, evolving gradually through later years on the SR, LMS and LNER, and carried to its ultimate extreme to the end of steam in BR days, when running plates were raised even higher and splashers disappeared completely

Nos 490 and 491 differed from the others in that they were at first unsuperheated, but by the time the photograph of No 491 was taken at Nine Elms in 1925 it had received a superheater and new type chimney

		No 491	Nos 482–90
Working Pressure (*lb psi*)		200	180
Heating Surface:			
Small Tubes	*sq ft*	1,252	1,252
Large Tubes	,,	464	464
Firebox	,,	162	167
Total	,,	1,878	1,883
Superheater	,,	337	337
Combined Total	,,	2,215	2,220
Grate Area	,,	28	30

Some of the engines were converted direct from Schmidt to 'Maunsell' superheater, and never had the 'Eastleigh' type at all. Examples were Nos 482/4/9, which retained the Schmidt apparatus until the 1930s. The 'Eastleigh' type appears to have been fitted first to No 491 (10/17), followed by 490 (12/19).

At Eastleigh in 1924 Maunsell built ten more engines of this class, with certain differences. As before the forward ring of the boiler was coned, but the running plate was carried level across the top of the steam chest, the cab cutaway was brought higher, and the Urie type of stovepipe chimney imparted a totally distinctive note. The tender, though fundamentally of the original design, was smaller (5,000 gallons and 5 tons), and had a correspondingly lower coping.

This lot weighed 79 tons 19cwt each, of which 58 tons 17cwt was adhesive.

They were fitted with an air pump, driven off the crosshead, for maintaining the vacuum in the train pipe of the braking system, and all except No 524 were built with 'Eastleigh' superheater. No 524 was the first engine of H15 Class to have a 'Maunsell' superheater incorporated as part of its original structure.

The above 20 units, in two lots, comprise the H15 Class proper, but in addition six other engines have been rebuilt to H15 standards, and are comprised in the total 26 units of the Class. These six accessions are Nos 330–4, nominally rebuilt from the Drummond engines of those numbers, but largely new constructions; and No 335, Urie's rebuild of Drummond's none-too-successful 4-cylinder 4-6-0, Class E14.

Referring to the latter first, No 335 was rebuilt at Eastleigh in November, 1914, as a 2-cylinder engine, with new outside cylinders and valve gear of the H15 design and layout. The old boiler was retained, suitably re-tubed for a 24-element 'Eastleigh' superheater, but the working pressure was kept at the original figure, 175lb. The following data apply to this engine as rebuilt.

Heating surface, small tubes 1,252sq ft, large tubes 464sq ft, firebox 168sq ft, superheater 308sq ft, combined total 2,192sq ft. Firebox 9ft 6in long outside, grate area 31·5sq ft. These figures have undergone modification due to the 'Maunsell' superheater, which yields 337sq ft of superheating surface, with a corresponding increase in the combined total to 2,221sq ft.

The weight (wo) of No 335 after the above conversion was 79 tons 12cwt, to which the 4,500 gallon Drummond inside-framed bogie tender added 49 tons, total 128 tons 12cwt.

The other five accessions, Nos 330–4, were turned out at Eastleigh 1924/5, and rank as 'Rebuilds' because the original boilers were re-used, as well as the

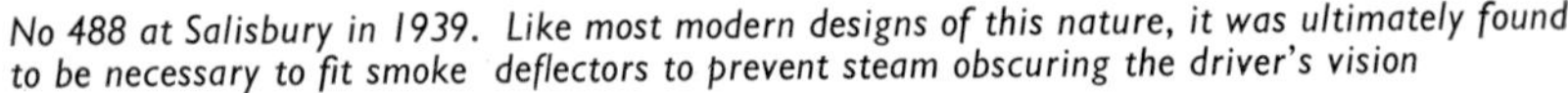
No 488 at Salisbury in 1939. Like most modern designs of this nature, it was ultimately found to be necessary to fit smoke deflectors to prevent steam obscuring the driver's vision

No 489 near Surbiton about 1926

No 491 by now as BR 30491, rebuilt with an N15 Class boiler and Maunsell superheater

Drummond inside-framed bogie tenders (capacity 3,700 gallons, since increased to 4,300 gallons). Though generally ranked with No 335, they differed from that engine in the minor point that the running plate was kept level from its front rise to its rear fall, and they were produced with 'Maunsell' superheaters.

The power class for the H15s was 'A'.

No	*Order No*	*Date*	*Works No*	*(M)*	*Wdn*	*No*	*Order No*	*Date*	*Works No*	*(M)*	*Wdn*
482	H.15–3	2/14	**40**	10/34	1959	475	R.16–3	3/24	**100**	6/30	1961
483	H.15–4	3/14	**41**	9/29	1957	476	R.16–4	4/24	**101**	1/29	1961
484	K.15–1	4/14	**43**	1/31	1959	477	R.16–5	5/24	**102**	12/29	1959
485	K.15–3	6/14	**45**	9/28	1955	478	T.16–1	6/24	**103**	5/30	1959
486	H.15–1	12/13	**38**	3/30	1959	521	T.16–2	7/24	**104**	9/29	1961
487	H.15–2	1/14	**39**	5/29	1957	522	T.16–3	,,	**105**	4/29	1961
488	H.15–5	3/14	**42**	3/28	1959	523	T.16–4	9/24	**106**	7/29	1961
489	K.15–2	5/14	**44**	3/32	1961	524	T.16–5	,,	**107**	*	1961
490	K.15–4	6/14	**46**	5/29	1955	330	A.17–1	10/24	**108**†	*	1957
491	K.15–5	7/14	**47**	6/27	1961	331	A.17–2	11/24	**109**†	*	1961
335	M.15–1	11/14	**48**†	12/27	1959	332	A.17–3	,,	**110**†	*	1956
473	R.16–1	2/24‡	**98**	11/31	1959	333	A.17–4	12/24	**111**†	*	1958
474	R.16–2	,,	**99**	6/31	1960	334	A.17–5	1/25	**112**†	*	1958

* 'Maunsell' superheater fitted when built.
† These engines are actually renewals of earlier engines.
‡ Dates and including this date onward are those when the engine was taken into stock. In most cases the engine would have been completed a few weeks before.
(M)—Date fitted with 'Maunsell' superheaters.
NOTE—Including No 335, which was an actual rebuild, No 475 was the 100th engine built at Eastleigh Works: the first one built there had been turned out 15 years before.
No 486 was taken into stock 1/14 and No 335 early in 1915.

The total of 26 H15 Class engines is thus made up of four distinct varieties which are, however, sufficiently alike to justify their inclusion in the one category.

N15 Class Express 4–6–0

Total in Urie class: 20. Built: LSWR (Eastleigh) 1918–23

These engines eventually found that group in the King Arthur Class known as the 'Urie Arthurs', and their design dates from 1917, when work was commenced on a new 4–6–0 express class developed from Urie's H15 mixed traffic engines which we have just noticed, but, owing to war conditions, the first engine was not put into traffic until the summer of 1918. They distinguished themselves for free steaming and general reliability. Historically, they are interesting because they were the first LSWR engines to have a taper boiler, but, contrary to policy largely established by the GWR, only the front boiler ring was tapered, and the second, or rearward, ring was made parallel.

Another novel feature introduced with these engines was the provision of steam cocks at the side of the smokebox with suitable means for connecting the tube-cleaning lances. This practice of cleaning the boiler tubes by jets of high-pressure steam was a feature also associated with Swindon.

The N15s were built with outside cylinders, 22in × 28in, with 11in piston valves, situated and actuated as in the H15s. The cylinders were later lined to a 21in bore, No 755 (BR 30755) excepted. Wheel diameter, bogie (engine and

In 1918 there appeared Urie's express version of the 4-6-0s, the 736 Class, subsequently perpetuated by Maunsell's well known King Arthurs, with which the Urie engines were eventually integrated. Nos 736-755, known as Class N15, were built between 1918 and 1923, and this view shows No 740 in original condition

No 739 is shown on a West of England express in Wandsworth cutting

tender), 3ft 7in, coupled 6ft 7in. Wheelbase, engine 7ft 6in + 5ft 6in + 7ft 0in + 7ft 6in, total 27ft 6in; tender, 19ft 0in, divided as already described under Class H15 heading; total (E&T) 58ft 0in. The boiler, pressed at 180lb and pitched 9ft 0in above rail, had a barrel of which the front ring tapered from 5ft 1$\frac{3}{4}$in minimum external diameter to an external diameter of 5ft 4$\frac{3}{4}$in at its junction with the second ring, which was 5ft 5$\frac{3}{4}$in external diameter and parallel. From tube plate to throat plate the barrel measured 13ft 9in. Power class, A.

The barrel contained 167 tubes, 2in external diameter, heating surface 1,252sq ft, and 24 5$\frac{1}{4}$in (external) tubes, heating surface 464sq ft, to which the firebox added 162sq ft, total water heating surface 1,878sq ft. An 'Eastleigh' superheater giving 308sq ft of surface brought the combined hs total to 2,186sq ft.

The firebox was 9ft 0in long outside, and the grate area 30sq ft. Over buffers, engine and tender measured 66ft 5$\frac{1}{4}$in. In working order, the engine weighed 77 tons 17cwt, of which 55 tons 19cwt rested on the coupled wheels, and the bogie tender added 57 tons 1cwt, giving a total weight (E&T) of 134 tons 18cwt.

In 1921, Nos 737 and 739 were converted—temporarily as it proved—to burn oil, and in 1947 several were similarly converted, including 740, 745, 748, 749, 752.

In later years, the 'Eastleigh' superheaters were replaced by those of the 'Maunsell' type, giving 337sq ft of superheating surface, which brought the combined total to 2,215sq ft. The Urie stovepipe chimneys were replaced, and in common with most modern express engines they had to be fitted with smokebox steam deflectors, to prevent the exhaust obscuring the driver's view.

No 743 Lyonesse *and 744* Maid of Astolat *passing one another near Tisbury in August 1940. Wartime shots at this time were difficult to obtain without danger of being arrested!*

No 740 Merlin temporarily fitted for oil burning in 1947

Some of these engines later received double blast pipes allied with wide chimneys. No 30736 Excalibur *at Clapham Junction in 1949*

The list of the 'Urie Arthurs' is as follows.

No	*Order No*	*Date*	*Works No*	*(M)*	*Wdn*	*No*	*Order No*	*Date*	*Works No*	*(M)*	*Wdn*
736	N.15–1	9/18	**49**	9/30	1956	746	L.16–1	6/22	**88**	1/29	1955
737	N.15–2	10/18	**50**	6/29	1956	747	L.16–2	7/22	**89**	11/30	1956
738	N.15–3	12/18	**51**	3/30	1958	748	L.16–3	8/22	**90**	11/29	1957
739	N.15–4	2/19	**52**	4/30	1957	749	L.16–4	9/22	**91**	12/28	1957
740	N.15–5	4/19	**53**	12/29	1955	750	L.16–5	10/22	**92**	2/30	1957
741	P.15–1	5/19	**54**	2/28	1956	751	N.16–1	11/22	**93**	6/29	1957
742	P.15–2	6/19	**55**	8/30	1957	752	N.16–2	12/22	**94**	9/30	1955
743	P.15–3	8/19	**56**	5/30	1955	753	N.16–3	,,	**95**	7/28	1957
744	P.15–4	9/19	**57**	1/30	1956	754	N.16–4	2/23	**96**	1/30	1953
745	P.15–5	11/19	**58**	1931	1956	755	N.16–5	3/23	**97**	3/29	1957

(M)—Date fitted with 'Maunsell' superheater.
No 753 was taken into stock 1/23.

Although the Southern Railway had come into existence before the order for the last lot was completed, all the engines were originally lettered LSWR, and painted in the modified livery, green with white lining and black edging, introduced by Urie. In LSWR days, they were not, of course, named, but when the SR decided to establish a range of nomenclature based on the legend of King Arthur, which is so intimately associated with districts served by the Western extremities of the system, the engines were fitted with cast brass nameplates as they passed through the shops. This work was done during 1925 and the list is as follows:

736	*Excalibur*	741	*Joyous Garad*	746	*Pendragon*	751	*Etarre*
737	*King Uther*	742	*Camelot*	747	*Elaine*	752	*Linette*
738	*King Pellinore*	743	*Lyonnesse*	748	*Vivien*	753	*Melisande*
739	*King Leodegrance*	744	*Maid of Astolat*	749	*Iseult*	754	*The Green Knight*
740	*Merlin*	745	*Tintagel*	750	*Morgan le Fay*	755	*The Red Knight*

The nameplate of No 755 was originally painted with a red ground, whereas the others had a black ground. The red background was afterwards adopted throughout. The above list does not, of course, include the complete range of names selected for the general group which eventually comprised 74 engines, numbered 448–457, 736–755, and 763–806.

S15 Class Mixed Traffic 4–6–0

Total in Urie class: 20. Built: LSWR (Eastleigh) 1920–1

For working fast freight and heavy passenger traffic, Urie put in service during 1920–1, 20 4–6–0 engines, Class S15, which were largely N15s with the coupled wheel diameter reduced to 5ft 7in, and the boiler pitched lower to suit. Here again, a long time elapsed between the drawings and the appearance of the first engine, and the design had already been completed during the latter part of 1917.

Apart from the driving wheel diameter, the principal dimensional differences between this class and the N15s were as follows. Cylinders, 21in × 28in. Engine wheelbase 7ft 6in + 5ft 4½in + 6ft 3in + 7ft 6in, total 26ft 7½in. A 5,000

In 1920 there appeared the first of another series of 4–6–0s, this time with 5ft 7in wheels, and the nearest thing the LSWR ever had to a heavy freight engine, but still of a design which could be, and often was, used on passenger work at peak holiday periods. Classified S15, they were numbered 496–515, and were built in 1920 and 1921. No 515, as first built

No 502, fitted with smoke deflectors, passing Vauxhall in 1932

gallon bogie tender of Urie's standard N15 type, brought the total wheelbase (E&T) to 57ft 1½in, and the total length over buffers to 65ft 6¾in. The boiler was pitched 8ft 7½in above rail, 4½in lower than that of the N15s, but with this exception, all the boiler data given under that heading apply to the present class.

The original weight (wo) of Class S15 was 21 tons 10cwt + 18 tons 4cwt + 19 tons 10cwt + 18 tons 4cwt, total 77 tons 8cwt, to which the tender added 57 tons 13cwt, bringing the total, (E&T) to 135 tons 1cwt.

The engines were equipped with 'Eastleigh' superheaters (which were replaced in after years), steam tube-cleaning equipment, and apparatus for carriage warming and had the vacuum brake complete.

In SR times, Maunsell added 25 more engines, with certain modifications, bringing the grand total of the class to 45. These additional engines were built in two lots, Nos 823–37 in 1927–8, and Nos 838–47 in 1936, and apart from this brief mention, they lie outside the scope of LSWR locomotive history.

A view of No 30498 near Battledown, Basingstoke, with freight train for Southampton Docks, in May, 1963

A view in 1960 at Feltham of 514 as British Railways' 30514, by now fitted with a Maunsell chimney

The list of the original S15s (power Class 'A') is as follows:

No	*Order No*	*Date*	*Works No*	*(M)*	*Wdn*	*No*	*Order No*	*Date*	*Works No*	*(M)*	*Wdn*
496	E.16–5	5/21	**78**	9/27	1963	506	A.16–5	10/20	**68**	2/30	1964
497	S.15–1	3/20	**59**	2/28	1963	507	C.16–1	11/20	**69**	1/32	1963
498	S.15–2	4/20	**60**	2/30	1963	508	C.16–2	12/20	**70**	8/29	1963
499	S.15–3	5/20	**61**	6/31	1964	509	C.16–3	,,	**71**	4/29	1963
500	S.15–4	,,	**62**	10/30	1963	510	C.16–4	1/21	**72**	2/31	1963
501	S.15–5	6/20	**63**	8/31	1963	511	C.16–5	,,	**73**	11/30	1963
502	A.16–1	7/20	**64**	5/30	1962	512	E.16–1	2/21	**74**	8/31	1964
503	A.16–2	8/20	**65**	5/31	1963	513	E.16–2	3/21	**75**	5/30	1963
504	A.16–3	9/20	**66**	1/29	1962	514	E.16–3	,,	**76**	5/31	1963
505	A.16–4	10/20	**67**	12/31	1962	515	E.16–4	4/21	**77**	9/31	1963

(M)—Date fitted with a Maunsell superheater.

The Urie S15s were always associated with the Feltham goods turns, and in 1942, no fewer than 16 of the original 20 were stationed at that depot, while the other four, Nos 496–9, were on loan to the GWR and had a GWR shed code stencilled on the angle iron.

No 515 is of interest because it was twice fitted to burn oil fuel, respectively in 1921 and 1926, but in each instance the apparatus was afterwards removed.

The reason that No 496 was the last one built lay in the fact that the Adams 0–6–0 bearing this number was still in service, and the necessity for placing it on the duplicate list as 0496 was thereby postponed for several months.

Later modifications included the usual chimney substitution and the provision of smokebox steam deflectors, also various tender changes.

No 492 at Strawberry Hill in 1921

G16 Class Hump Shunting 4–8–0T

Total in class: 4. Built: LSWR (Eastleigh) 1921

This class comprises four side-tank engines built by Urie for working the 'hump' or gravitation sorting sidings at the then newly opened Feltham marshalling yard, and for dealing with transfer traffic between Feltham and Nine Elms Goods Station.

With their high tractive force of 33,990lb (at 85 per cent. bp), these were amongst the most powerful tank engines in England, and they looked the part, with their sharply dropped running plate, steeply inclined cylinders, and raked tank ends—the latter for the sake of improving the drivers' look out. The raked ends give the curious illusion that the boiler barrel is tapered as in the Urie N15 Class, but such is not the case. It is made in two parallel rings, respectively 4ft 10¾in and 5ft 0in external diameters, and is 12ft 0in long from tube plate to throat plate.

The boilers of these engines, and those of the H16 tanks presently to be noticed, are a type on their own, and are not interchangeable with any class of engine other than these two Groups of Urie tanks. Pitched 9ft above rail, and pressed at 180lb, they are tubed with 158 1¾in tubes yielding 910sq ft heating surface, and 21 5¼in superheater flues yielding 357sq ft, to which the firebox adds 139sq ft, total water surface 1,406sq ft. Originally, an 'Eastleigh' superheater provided 231sq ft of superheating surface, which brought the combined total to 1,637sq ft, but the superheaters of that type were later replaced by those of the 'Maunsell' providing 252sq ft, and increasing the combined total to 1,658sq ft.

The G16 Class had two outside cylinders, 22 × 28in, with Urie's customary steam distribution, and cylinders and motion are interchangeable with those of the N15 Class, but in the G16s, the cylinders are more steeply inclined. The other leading dimensions are as follows:

Wheel diameter, bogie 3ft 7in, coupled 5ft 1in. Wheelbase, 7ft 6in + 6ft 6in + 6ft 0in + 6ft 0in + 6ft 0in, total 32ft 0in. Firebox length, 8ft 4in outside, grate area 27sq ft. Over buffers 42ft 10¼in. Tank capacity, 2,000 gallons, coal capacity 3½ tons. The weight in working order is 95 tons 2cwt, of which 72 tons 18cwt, distributed 18 tons 9cwt + 18 tons 10cwt + 18 tons 9cwt + 17 tons 10cwt, is carried on the coupled wheels.

The height over chimney (which was of Urie's standard 'stovepipe' pattern), is the customary 13ft 2¾in, and the maximum width of the engine, 9ft 2in, entitles the G16s to rank with the T14s and the H16s as the widest locomotives in the country.

The G16s were fitted with steam brake and vacuum ejector. No radical change was made in their structure or appearance during their 40 odd years of service. They were classed A for power.

No	*Order No*	*Date*	*Works No*	*(M)*	*Wdn*
492	G.16–1	7/21	**79**	5/30	1959
493	G.16–2	,,	**80**	7/31	1959
494	G.16–3	8/21	**81**	12/29	1962
495	G.16–4	,,	**82**	3/30	1962

H16 Class Goods 4–6–2T

Total in class: 5. Built: LSWR (Eastleigh) 1921–2

For working the interchange traffic between Brent sidings, Midland Railway, and Feltham Yard, and between Willesden (LNWR) and Feltham Yard, Urie built these five 4–6–2 tank engines, Class H16, the trailing axle of which was mounted in a radial truck. Turned out immediately after the 4–8–0 tanks just described, the H16 engines had identical dimensions wherever possible, and, except that the cylinders were made 21in diameter instead of 22in, whatever differences existed were largely dictated by the different wheel arrangement. An interesting example, not externally obvious, was the ashpan which could be made much longer in virtue of the wider spacing of the rearward coupled wheels. Also, the side tanks were made long and low, which obviated the necessity to rake their front ends while keeping their water capacity unchanged.

4–6–2T No 516 at Strawberry Hill, 1921

4–8–0T No 495 shunting over the hump at Feltham in 1924

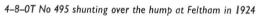

No 518 working Waterloo–Ascot Race Special in SR days

No 30520 with the empty stock of the Bournemouth Belle near Queen's Road, Battersea, 1958

Apart from the cylinder diameter noted above, the following dimensions are the only ones of any importance in which the H16s differed from the G16s. The radial and bogie wheels are of the customary diameter, 3ft 7in; coupled wheel diameter, 5ft 7in. Wheelbase, 7ft 6in + 6ft 0in + 6ft 6in + 8ft 6in + 8ft 0in total 36ft 6in. Over buffers, 46ft 0in. Weight in working order, 96 tons 8cwt (26cwt more than the G16s), of which 59 tons, distributed 19 tons 16cwt + 19 tons 12cwt + 19 tons 12cwt, is on the coupled wheels, and 15 tons is on the trailing radial axle. Power class, A.

The H16 engines were fitted with steam brake and vacuum ejector; they were not classed for power. Although primarily intended for the short-distance work indicated above, they were occasionally seen on special and semi-fast passenger trains. They were also used on race specials during Ascot week.

No	*Order No*	*Date*	*Works No*	*(M)*	*Wdn*
516	H.16–1	11/21	**83**	8/29	1962
517	H.16–2	,,	**84**	5/29	1962
518	H.16–3	12/21	**85**	3/29	1962
519	H.16–4	1/22	**86**	4/28	1962
520	H.16–5	2/22	**87**	12/29	1962

(M)—Date fitted with Maunsell superheater.

Like their 4–8–0T counterparts, these 4–6–2Ts remained practically unaltered during their 40 years' existence.

The H16 tanks were Urie's last class for the LSWR, and on the formation of the Southern Railway he retired, handing over to R. E. L. Maunsell a group of eminently sound designs that profoundly influenced the new CME's progress.

CHAPTER SEVEN

OTHER ENGINES

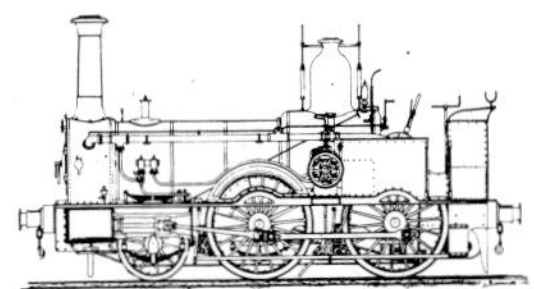

To HELP alleviate the shortage of engines resulting from the despatch of 50 Adams 0–6–0s abroad in World War I, the LSWR had to borrow some 0–6–0s from the Great Northern and Midland, and also after the cessation of hostilities some Robinson 2–8–0s from the War Department. Although never taken officially into stock in the sense of receiving LSWR initials or numbers, they nevertheless worked for three years, from 1917 to 1920, as South Western engines.

GNR Stirling 0–6–0 No 150A, one of several which worked for three years on the LSWR, at Strawberry Hill in 1920

MR No 2785 was one of three which worked as LSWR engines between 1917 and 1920. Unfortunately no photographs of it working on the South Western seem to have been taken, or at any rate survived, and this picture was taken some years later at Derby after it had been repainted LMS. The brass plate on the cabside reads 'This engine was on loan to the R.O.D. France, 1917–1919', although in fact it never crossed the Channel

WD 2–8–0 No 1733 at Strawberry Hill in 1920

PD&SWJR 0–6–0T A. S. Harris *as first repainted in 1923. It later received the number E756. Built by Hawthorn Leslie in 1907 (works No 2697) it ran until 1951. Although allocated BR No 30756 it never carried it*

The two 0–6–2Ts were Earl of Mount Edgecumbe *and* Lord St Levan; *Hawthorn Leslie 1907 (2696 and 2695). They became SR Nos E757 and E758 and eventually BR 30757 and 30758, and were scrapped in 1957*

The GNR engines were of Stirling design, Nos 150A, 192, 304, 312, 846, 1087 and 1131. Most of them worked from Strawberry Hill shed. The Midland's were three elderly double framed 0–6–0s, Nos 2783–2785, built by Neilson in 1872, not unlike the LSWR's own Beattie engines of the same period and with which they could now be seen alongside. They were part of a large consignment of about 80 engines appropriated by the War Department for use in France, but somehow these three never reached there, being in some way stopped by the LSWR on their way south and retained for its own use. They did nevertheless manage to acquire brass cabside plates on their return to Derby, in common with the rest of the batch, commemorating their service in France, the Midland Railway authority themselves apparently unaware of the fact that they never crossed the Channel! They spent most of their sojourn at Guildford.

The 2–8–0s, of Robinson's GCR design, which had been adopted by the War Department as standard type, and which were built in large numbers, did not arrive on the LSWR until 1919. There were at least 18 of them, Nos 1733, 1738–1742, 1744, 1745, 2069–2072 and 2119–2124 (and there may have been one or two others, unrecorded). It was intended at one time to give them numbers from 800 upwards in the LSWR list, but this was never done, and they were disposed of in 1920; some went to the LNWR and GWR, whilst three of them travelled to the other side of the world to work at a colliery in New South Wales. On the South Western they were stationed principally at Strawberry Hill and Salisbury sheds.

A small and nominally independent railway until the 1923 Grouping was the Plymouth, Devonport & South Western Junction, actually the owners of the section of main line between Bere Alston and Devonport, which was leased to and worked by the LSWR as part of its own system. The branch from Bere Alston to Callington was worked by the PD&SWJR on its own account, for which they latterly possessed three engines, a 0–6–0T and two 0–6–2Ts. Although not absorbed until 1923, when they became in effect SR engines. they appeared at first with the initials LSWR on the side tanks, as it was not until several months after the amalgamation that the word *Southern* began to appear on the locomotives.

Four generations at Bournemouth shed in 1928: King Arthur No E790 (Maunsell's developed Urie design); Maunsell 2–6–0 A834; Adams 4–4–0 E580, and Drummond 4–4–0 E156

APPENDIX

SOME WORKS AND SHED SCENES

LSWR electric locomotive at Durnsford Road Power Station

An old Beattie tender converted to a travelling tar tank, under repair at Three Bridges in 1926

Eastleigh Works after transfer from Nine Elms in 1910

A view in the paint shop taken in 1927

A part of Eastleigh yard in 1921, showing No 0419

Eastleigh scrap siding in 1933, showing Nos 581, 568, 656, 662, B298, B217, 341, 333

View in the erecting shops in 1930

1947 line of engines awaiting entry into works; 'Grasshopper' 388 in foreground

Exmouth Junction old shed in 1925; the following year it was replaced by a modern structure built at the rear

The picturesque setting of Yeovil shed with a line of engines; a view taken in 1926

ACKNOWLEDGEMENTS

Due acknowledgement is given for authorship of photographs, where known, but some early ones have had to remain anonymous.

Most of the uncredited illustrations which can be identified as dating from 1920 onwards are from the author's own negatives.

Copyright is held by the undermentioned people for the photographs appearing on the pages listed:

W. Benson:	lower photograph on page 75
R. J. Buckley:	lower—62
R. M. Casserley:	bottom—123
L. Elsey:	lower—156
R. K. Evans:	169
D. J. Morris:	96; upper left—128, and 136
E. Pouteau:	lower—138
R. C. Riley:	44; bottom—53; lower—97; bottom—109; 168, and lower—173
A. Trickett:	lower—161

It is not possible to illustrate (other than by contemporary engravings) anything of the earliest period, as photography, except on a very primitive experimental basis, did not become a practical proposition until several years after the formation of the LSWR, and was a slow and cumbersome process for a long time until the development of the dry plate in the 1870s. Even then the speed of the emulsion was very slow and it was not until the 1890s that it became possible to photograph a moving object such as a train in motion.

Largely owing to the fine efforts of that indefatigable pioneer of railway photography, R. E. Bleasdale, who did such yeoman work in this direction between the 1860s and 1890s, there are many photographs of the locomotives in use over the period, the negatives of which are still in existence and held by the present publishers. Some of these are included in the present volume.

No 332 thunders into Crewkerne Tunnel; August 1928